CAMBRIDGE LIBRARY COLLECTION

Books of enduring scholarly value

History

The books reissued in this series include accounts of historical events and movements by eye-witnesses and contemporaries, as well as landmark studies that assembled significant source materials or developed new historiographical methods. The series includes work in social, political and military history on a wide range of periods and regions, giving modern scholars ready access to influential publications of the past.

The Conquest of Siberia

Gerhard Müller (1705–1783) is renowned as the first historian to specialise in the history and culture of Siberia. Born in Westphalia, Müller was invited to teach at the newly founded Academy of Sciences in St. Petersburg in 1725. He joined the Second Kamtchatka Expedition to western Siberia in 1735, and on his return spent the remainder of his life publishing works on the history of Siberia. His co-author Peter Simon Pallas (1741–1811) also served on several expeditions to Siberia. This volume, first published in English in 1842, contains the English translation of these authors' detailed description of the Russian colonisation of Siberia and tensions with China. Combining ethnographic material with accounts of Russia's trade with indigenous Siberian peoples and China, this volume presented one of the first scholarly accounts of Siberia to western Europe at a time when the region was little known outside of Russia.

T0371272

The Conquest
of Siberia

*And the History of the Transactions, Wars,
Commerce, &c. &c. Carried on between
Russia and China, from the Earliest Period*

GERHARD FRIEDRICH MÜLLER
PETER SIMON PALLAS

CAMBRIDGE
UNIVERSITY PRESS

CAMBRIDGE UNIVERSITY PRESS

Cambridge, New York, Melbourne, Madrid, Cape Town, Singapore,
São Paolo, Delhi, Dubai, Tokyo, Mexico City

Published in the United States of America by Cambridge University Press, New York

www.cambridge.org
Information on this title: www.cambridge.org/9781108023832

© in this compilation Cambridge University Press 2010

This edition first published 1842
This digitally printed version 2010

ISBN 978-1-108-02383-2 Paperback

THE

CONQUEST OF SIBERIA,

AND THE HISTORY OF THE

TRANSACTIONS, WARS, COMMERCE, &c. &c.

CARRIED ON BETWEEN

RUSSIA AND CHINA,

FROM THE EARLIEST PERIOD.

CONQUEST OF SIBERIA,

AND THE HISTORY OF THE

TRANSACTIONS, WARS, COMMERCE,

&c. &c.

CARRIED ON BETWEEN

RUSSIA AND CHINA,

FROM THE EARLIEST PERIOD.

TRANSLATED FROM THE RUSSIAN OF

G. F. MULLER,

HISTORIOGRAPHER OF RUSSIA, AND OF

PETER SIMON PALLAS, M.D. F.R.S.

COUNSELLOR OF THE BOARD OF MINES TO THE
EMPRESS OF RUSSIA,

MEMBER OF THE IMPERIAL ACADEMY OF SCIENCES AT SAINT
PETERSBURGH, ETC. ETC.

London:

SMITH, ELDER, AND CO. CORNHILL.

PRINTED BY GEO. NICHOLS, EARL'S COURT, LEICESTER SQUARE.

1842.

EXPLANATION

OF

SOME RUSSIAN WORDS MADE USE OF IN THE FOLLOWING WORK.

Baidar, a small boat.
Guba, a bay.
Kamen, a rock.
Kotche, a vessel.
Krepost, a regular fortress.
Noss, a cape.
Ostrog, a fortress surrounded with pallisadoes.
Ostroff, an island.
Ostrova, islands.
Quass, a sort of fermented liquor.
Reka, a river.

The Russians, in their proper names of persons, make use of patronymics; these patronymics are formed in some cases by adding *Vitch* to the christian name of the father; in others, *Off* or *Eff;* the former termination is applied only to persons of condition; the latter to those of an inferior rank. As, for instance,

Among persons of condition — *Ivan Ivanovitch* } Ivan the son
  of inferior rank, *Ivan Ivanoff* } of Ivan.

  Michael Alexievitch, } Michael the son
  Michael Alexeff, } of Alexèy.

Sometimes a surname is added, Ivan Ivanovitch Romanoff.

TABLE

OF

RUSSIAN WEIGHTS, MEASURES OF LENGTH,

AND

VALUE OF MONEY.

WEIGHT.

A pood weighs 40 Russian pounds—36 English.

MEASURES OF LENGTH.

16 vershocks — an arsheen.

An arsheen — 28 inches.

Three arsheens, or seven feet — a fathom,* or sazshen.

500 sazshens — a verst.

A degree of longitude comprises $104\frac{1}{2}$ versts — $69\frac{1}{2}$ English miles. A mile is therefore 1,515 parts of a verst; two miles may then be estimated equal to three versts, omitting a small fraction.

VALUE OF RUSSIAN MONEY.

A rouble — 100 copecs.

Its value varies according to the exchange, from 3s. 8d. to 4s. 2d. Upon an average, however, the value of a rouble is reckoned at four shillings.

---

* The fathom for measuring the depth of water is the same as the English fathom — 6 feet.

CONTENTS.

CHAP. I.

SIBERIA was scarcely known to the Russians before the middle of the sixteenth century. For although an expedition was made, under the reign of Ivan Vassilievitch I. into the north-western parts of that country, as far as the river Oby, by which several Tartar tribes were rendered tributary, and some of their chiefs brought prisoners to Moscow; yet this incursion bore a greater resemblance to the desultory inroads of barbarians, than to any permanent establishment of empire by a civilized nation. Indeed

the effects of that expedition soon vanished;
nor does any trace of the least communication
with Siberia again appear in the Russian history
before the reign of Ivan Vassilievitch II. At
that period Siberia again became an object of
attention, by means of one Anika Strogonoff, a
Russian merchant, who had established some
salt works at Solvytshegodskaia, a town in the
government of Archangel.

This person carried on a trade of barter with
the inhabitants of the north-western parts of
Siberia, who brought every year to the above-
mentioned town large quantities of the choicest
furs. Upon their return to their country, Strogonoff was accustomed to send with them some
Russian merchants, who crossed the mountains,
and traded with the natives. By these means a
considerable number of very valuable furs were
procured at an easy rate, in exchange for toys
and other commodities of trifling value.

This traffic was continued for several years,
without any interruption, during which Strogonoff

rapidly amassed a very considerable fortune. At length the Czar Ivan Vassilievitch II. foreseeing the advantages which would accrue to his subjects, from establishing · a more general and regular commerce with these people, determined to enlarge the communication already opened with Siberia. Accordingly he sent a corps of troops into that country. They followed the same route which had been discovered by the Russians in the former expedition, and which was lately frequented by the merchants of Solvytshegodskaia. It lay along the banks of the Petschora, and from thence crossed the Yugorian mountains, which form the north-eastern boundary of Europe. These troops, however, do not seem to have passed the Irtish, or to have penetrated further than the western branch of the river Oby. Some Tartar tribes were indeed laid under contribution; and a chief, whose name was Yediger, consented to pay an annual tribute of a thousand sables. But this expedition was not productive of any lasting effects; for soon afterwards Yediger was defeated, and taken prisoner by Kutchum Chan; the latter was a lineal descendant of the celebrated Zinghis Chan, and had newly established his empire in those parts.

This second inroad was probably made about the middle of the sixteenth century; for the Czar Ivan Vassilievitch assumed the title of Lord of all the Siberian lands so early as 1558, before the conquests made by Yermac in that kingdom. But probably the name of Siberia was at that time only confined to the district then rendered tributary; and as the Russians extended their conquests, this appellation was afterwards applied to the whole tract of country which now bears that name.

For some time after the above-mentioned expedition, the Czar does not appear to have made any attempts towards recovering his lost authority in those distant regions. But his attention was again turned to that quarter by a concurrence of incidents; which, though begun without his immediate interposition, terminated in a vast accession of territory.

Strogonoff, in recompense for having first opened a trade with the inhabitants of Siberia, obtained from the Czar large grants of land; accordingly he founded colonies upon the banks of the rivers Kama and Tchussovaia; and these settlements gave rise to the entire subjection of Siberia, by the refuge which they not long afterwards afforded to Yermac Timofeeff.

This person was nothing more than a fugitive Cossack of the Don, and chief of a troop of banditti who infested the shores of the Caspian Sea. But as he was the instrument by which such a vast extent of dominion was added to the Russian empire, it will not be uninteresting to develop the principal circumstances, which brought this Cossack from the shores of the Caspian to the banks of the Kama; and to trace the progress which he afterwards made in the distant regions of Siberia.

By the victories which the Czar Ivan Vassilie-vitch had gained over the Tartars of Casan and Astracan, that monarch extended his dominions

as far as the Caspian Sea; and thereby established a commerce with the Persians and
Bucharians. But as the merchants who traded
to those parts were continually pillaged by the
Cossacks of the Don; and as the roads which
lay by the side of that river, and of the Volga,
were infested with those banditti, the Czar sent
a considerable force against them. Accordingly,
they were attacked and routed; part were slain,
part made prisoners, and the rest escaped by
flight. Among the latter was a corps of six
thousand Cossacks, under the command of the
above-mentioned Yermac Timofeeff.

That celebrated adventurer, being driven from
his usual haunts, retired, with his followers, into
the interior part of the province of Casan.
From thence he directed his course along the
banks of the Kama, until he came to Orel.
That place was one of the Russian settlements
recently planted, and was governed by Maxim,
grandson of Anika Strogonoff. Yermac, instead
of storming the place, and pillaging the inhabitants, acted with a degree of moderation

unusual in a chief of banditti. Being hospitably received by Strogonoff, and supplied with every thing necessary for the subsistence of his troops, he fixed his winter quarters at that settlement. His restless genius, however, did not suffer him to continue for any length of time in a state of inactivity; and from the intelligence he procured concerning the situation of the neighbouring Tartars of Siberia, he turned his arms toward that quarter.

Siberia was at that time partly divided among a number of separate princes; and partly inhabited by the various tribes of independent Tartars. Of the former, Kutchum Chan was the most powerful sovereign. His dominions consisted of that tract of country which now forms the south-western part of the province of Tobolsk; and stretched from the banks of the Irtish and Oby to those of the Tobol and Tura. His principal residence was at Sibir*, a small fortress

---

* Several authors have supposed the name of Siberia to derive its origin from this fortress, soon after it was first taken by the Russians under Yermac. But this opinion is advanced

upon the river Irtish, not far from the present
town of Tobolsk, and of which some ruins are
still to be seen. Although his power was very
considerable, yet there were some circumstances
which seemed to ensure success to an enterprising
invader. He had newly acquired a large part of
his territories by conquest; and had, in a great
measure, alienated the affections of his idolatrous
subjects, by the intolerant zeal with which he
introduced and desseminated the Mahometan
religion.

Strogonoff did not fail of displaying to Yermac
this inviting posture of affairs, as well with the
view of removing him from his present station,
as because he himself was personally exasperated
against Kutchum Chan; for the latter had

without sufficient foundation; for the name   of Siber · was
unknown to the Tartars, that fort being by them called Isker.
Besides, the southern part of the province of Tobolsk, to
which the name of Siberia was originally applied, was thus
denominated by the Russians before the invasion of Yermac.
This denomination probably first came from the Permians and
Sirjanians, who brought the first accounts of Siberia to the
Russians.

secretly instigated a large body of Tartars to
invade the Russian settlements upon the river
Tchussovaia; and had afterwards commenced
open hostilities against them with a body of
forces under the command of his cousin Mehemet
Kul. And although both these attempts had
failed of success, yet the troops engaged in them
had left behind traces of havoc and devastation
too lasting to be easily effaced.

All these various considerations were not lost
upon Yermac: having, therefore, employed the
winter in preparations for his intended expedition, he began his march in the summer of
the following year, 1578, along the banks of the
Tchussovaia. The want of proper guides, and a
neglect of other necessary precautions, greatly
retarded his march, and he was overtaken by
the winter before he had made any considerable
progress. And at the appearance of spring he
found his stock of provisions so nearly exhausted,
that he was reduced to the necessity of returning
to Orel.

But this failure of success by no means extinguished his ardour for the prosecution of the enterprise; it only served to make him still more solicitous in guarding against the possibility of a future miscarriage. By threats he extorted from Strogonoff every assistance which the nature of the expedition seemed to require. Besides a sufficient quantity of provisions, all his followers, who were before unprovided with fire-arms, were supplied with muskets and ammunition; and, in order to give the appearance of a regular army to his troops, colours were distributed to each company, which were ornamented with the images of saints, after the manner of the Russians.

Having thus made all previous arrangements, he thought himself in a condition to force his way into Siberia. Accordingly, in the month of June, 1579, he set out upon this second expedition. His followers amounted to five thousand men; adventurers inured to hardships, and regardless of danger: they placed implicit confidence in their leader, and seemed to be all animated with one and the same spirit. He continued his route partly by land, and partly by water: the navigation, however, of the rivers was so tedious, and the roads so rugged and difficult, that eighteen months elapsed before he reached Tchingi, a small town upon the banks of the Tura.

Here he mustered his troops, and found his army considerably reduced: part had been exhausted by fatigue, part carried off by sickness, and part cut off in skirmishes with the Tartars. The whole remaining number amounted to about fifteen hundred effective men; and yet with this handful of troops Yermac did not hesitate a moment in advancing against Kutchum Chan. That prince was already in a posture of defence; and resolved to guard his crown to the last extremity. Having collected his forces, he dispatched several flying parties against Yermac, himself remaining behind with the flower of his troops: but all these detachments were driven back with considerable loss; and worsted in many successive skirmishes. Yermac continued his march without intermission, bearing down all resistance until he reached the centre of his adversary's dominions.

These successes, however, were dearly bought; for his army was now reduced to five hundred men. Kutchum Chan was encamped* at no great distance upon the banks of the Irtish, with a very superior force, and determined to give him battle. Yermac, who was not to be daunted by the inequality of numbers, prepared for the engagement with a confidence which never forsook him; his troops were equally impatient for action, and knew no medium between conquest and death. The event of the combat corresponded with this magnanimity. After an obstinate and well-fought battle, victory declared in favour of Yermac: the Tartars were entirely routed, and the carnage was so general, that Kutchum Chan himself escaped with difficulty.

---

* The place where the Tartar army lay encamped was called Tschuvatch: it is a neck of land washed by the Irtish, near the spot where the Tobol falls into that river.

This defeat proved decisive : Kutchum Chan was deserted by his subjects ; and Yermac, who knew how to improve as well as gain a victory, marched without delay to Sibir, the residence of the Tartar princes. He was well aware, that the only method to secure his conquest was to get possession of that important fortress. He expected therefore to have found in that place a considerable garrison, determined to sacrifice their lives in its defence. But the news of the late defeat had diffused universal consternation, and Sibir was entirely deserted. A body of troops whom he sent before him, to reduce the fortress, found it quite deserted: he himself soon after made his triumphal entry, and seated himself upon the throne without the least opposition. Here he fixed his residence, and received the allegiance of the neighbouring people, who poured in from all quarters upon the news of this unexpected revolution. The Tartars were so struck with his gallant intrepidity and brilliant exploits, that they submitted to his authority without hesitation, and acquiesced in the payment of the usual tribute.

Thus this enterprising Cossack was suddenly exalted from the station of a chief of banditti to the rank of a sovereign prince. It does not appear from history whether it were at first his design to conquer Siberia, or solely to amass a considerable booty. The latter, indeed, seems the most probable conjecture. The rapid tide of success with which he was carried on, and the entire defeat of Kutchum Chan, afterwards expanded his views, and opened a larger scene to his ambition. But whatever were his original projects, he seems worthy, so far as intrepidity and prudence form a basis of merit, of the final success which flowed in upon him; for he was neither elated with unexpected prosperity, nor dazzled with the sudden glare of royalty: on the contrary, the dignity of his deportment was as consistent and unaffected, as if he had been born a sovereign.

And now Yermac and his followers seemed to enjoy those rewards which they had dearly purchased by a course of unremitted fatigue, and by victories which almost exceeded belief.

Not only the tribes in the neighbourhood of Sibir wore the appearance of the most unreserved submission; but even princes continued flocking in from distant parts, to acknowledge themselves tributary, and to claim his protection. However, this calm was of short duration. Insurrections were concerted by Kutchum Chan; who, though driven from his dominions, yet still retained no small degree of influence over his former subjects.

Yermac saw and felt the precariousness of his present grandeur; the inconsiderable number of his followers who had survived the conquest of Sibir, had been still further diminished by an ambuscade of the enemy; and as he could not depend on the affection of his new subjects, he found himself under the necessity either of calling in foreign assistance, or of relinquishing his dominion. Under these circumstances he had recourse to the Czar of Muscovy; and made a tender of his new acquisitions to that monarch, upon condition of receiving immediate and effectual support. The judicious manner in

which he conducted this measure, shows him
no less able in the arts of negociation than
of war.

One of his most confidential followers was
dispatched to Moscow at the head of fifty Cossacks. He had orders to represent to the court
the progress which the Russian troops, under
the command of Yermac, had made in Siberia :
he was artfully to add, that an extensive empire
was conquered in the name of the Czar ; that
the natives were reduced to swear allegiance to
that monarch, and consented to pay an annual
tribute. This representation was accompanied
with a present of the choicest and most valuable
furs. The ambassador was received at Moscow
with the strongest marks of satisfaction : a public
thanksgiving was celebrated in the cathedral ;
the Czar acknowledged and extolled the good
services of Yermac ; he granted him a pardon
for all former offences ; and, as a testimony of
his favour, distributed presents for him and his
followers. Amongst those which were sent to
Yermac was a fur robe, which the Czar himself

had worn, and which was the greatest mark of distinction that could be conferred upon a subject. To these was added a sum of money, and a promise of speedy and effectual assistance.

Meanwhile Yermac, notwithstanding the inferior number of his troops, did not remain inactive within the fortress of Sibir. He defeated all attempts of Kutchum Chan to recover his crown; and took his principal general prisoner. He made occasional inroads into the adjacent provinces, and extended his conquests up to the source of the river Taffda on one side, and on the other as far as the district which lies upon the river Oby above its junction with the Irtish.

At length the promised succours arrived at Sibir. They consisted of five hundred Russians, under the command of Prince Bolkosky, who was appointed wayvode or governer of Siberia. Strengthened by this reinforcement, Yermac continued his excursions on all sides with his usual activity; and gained several bloody victories over different princes, who were imprudent enough to assert their independence.

In one of these expeditions he laid siege to
Kullara, a small fortress upon the banks of the
Irtish, which still belonged to Kutchum Chan:
but he found it so bravely defended by that
monarch, that all his efforts to carry it by storm
proved ineffectual. Upon his return to Sibir,
he was followed at some distance by that prince,
who hung unperceived upon his rear: and was
prepared to sieze any fortunate moment of attack
which might occur: nor was it long before a
favourable opportunity presented itself. The
Russians to the number of about three hundred
lay negligently posted in a small island, formed
by two branches of the Irtish. The night was
obscure and rainy; and the troops, who were
fatigued with a long march, reposed themselves
without suspicion of danger. Kutchum Chan,
apprised of their situation, silently advanced at
midnight with a select body of troops; and
having forded the river, came with such rapidity
upon the Russians, as to preclude the use of
their arms. In the darkness and confusion of
the night, the latter were cut to pieces almost
without opposition; and fell a resistless prey to
those adversaries, whom they had been accus-

tomed to conquer and despise. The massacre
was so universal, that only one man is recorded
to have escaped, and to have brought the news
of this catastrophe to his countrymen at Sibir.

Yermac himself perished in the rout, though
he did not fall by the sword of the enemy. In
all the hurry of surprise, he was not so much
infected with the general panic, as to forget his
usual intrepidity, which seemed to be increased
rather than abated by the danger of his present
situation. After many desperate acts of heroism,
he cut his way through the troops who surrounded him, and made to the banks of the
Irtish.* Being closely pursued by a detachment
of the enemy, he endeavoured to throw himself
into a boat which lay near the shore; but step-

---

* Many difficulties have arisen concerning the branch of the
Irtish in which Yermac was drowned; but it is now sufficiently
ascertained that it was a canal, which some time before this
catastrophe had been cut by order of that Cossack: not far
from the spot, where the Vagai falls into the Irtish, the latter
river forms a bend of six versts; by cutting a canal in a
straight line from the two extreme points of this sweep, he
shortened the length of the navigation.

ping short, he fell into the water, and being encumbered with the weight of his armour, sunk instantly to the bottom.*

His body was not long afterwards taken out of the Irtish, and exposed, by order of Kutchum Chan, to all the insults which revenge ever suggested to barbarians in the frenzy of success. But these first transports of resentment had no sooner subsided, than the Tartars testified the most pointed indignation at the ungenerous ferocity of their leader. The prowess of Yermac, his consummate valour and magnanimity, virtues which barbarians know how to prize, rose upon their recollection. They made a sudden tran-

---

* Cyprian was appointed the first archbishop of Siberia, in 1621. Upon his arrival at Tobolsk, he enquired for several of the ancient followers of Yermac who were still alive; and from them he made himself acquainted with the principal circumstances attending the expedition of that Cossack, and the conquest of Siberia. Those circumstances he transmitted to writing; and these papers are the archives of the Siberian history; from which the several historians of that country have drawn their relations. Sava Yesimoff, who was himself one of Yermac's followers, is one of the most accurate historians of those times. He carries down his history to the year 1636.

sition from one extreme to the other: they reproached their leader for ordering, themselves for being the instruments of indignity to such venerable remains. At length their heated imaginations proceeded even to consecrate his memory: they interred his body with all the rites of Pagan superstition, and offered up sacrifices to his manes.

Many stories were soon spread abroad, and met with implicit belief. The touch of his body was supposed to have been an instantaneous cure for all disorders; and even his clothes and arms were said to be endowed with the same efficacy. A flame of fire was represented as sometimes hovering about his tomb, and sometimes as stretching in one luminous body from the same spot towards the heavens. A presiding influence over the affairs of the chace and of war was attributed to his departed spirit; and numbers resorted to his tomb to invoke his tutelary aid in concerns so interesting to uncivilized nations. These idle fables, though they evince the superstitious credulity of the Tartars, convey at the same time the strongest testimony of their

veneration for the memory of Yermac ; and this
veneration greatly contributed to the subsequent
progress of the Russians in those regions.*

With Yermac expired for a time the Russian
empire in Siberia. The news of his defeat and
death no sooner reached the garrison of Sibir,
than an hundred and fifty troops, the sad remains of that formidable army which had gained
such a series of almost incredible victories, retired from the fortress, and evacuated Siberia.
Notwithstanding this disaster, the court of Moscow did not abandon its design upon that
country; which a variety of favorable circumstances still concurred to render a flattering object
of Russian ambition. Yermac's sagacity had

---

* Even so late as the middle of the next century, this
veneration for the memory of Yermac had not subsided.   Allai,
a powerful prince of the Calmucs, is said to have been cured
of a dangerous disorder, by mixing some earth taken from
Yermac's tomb in water, and drinking the infusion.   That prince
is also reported to have carried with him a small portion of the
same earth, whenever he engaged in any important enterprise.
This earth he superstitiously considered as a kind of charm;
and was persuaded that he always secured a prosperous issue
to his affairs by this precaution.

discovered new and commodious routes for the march of troops across those inhospitable regions. The rapidity with which he had overrun the territories of Kutchum Chan, taught the Russians to consider the Tartars as an easy prey. Many of the tribes who had been rendered tributary by Yermac, had testified a cheerful acquiescence under the sovereignty of the Czar; and were inclined to renew their allegiance upon the first opportunity. Others looked upon all resistance as unavailing, and had learned, from dear-bought experience, to tremble at the very name of a Russian. The natural strength of the country, proved not to be irresistible when united, was considerably weakened by its intestine commotions. Upon the retreat of the garrison of Sibir, that fortress, together with the adjacent district, was seized by Seyidyak, son of the former sovereign, whom Kutchum Chan had dethroned and put to death. Other princes availed themselves of the general confusion to assert independency; and Kutchum Chan was able to regain only a small portion of those dominions, of which he had been stripped by Yermac.

Influenced by these motives, the court of Moscow, sent a body of three hundred troops into Siberia, who penetrated to the banks of the Tura as far as Tschingi almost without opposition. There they built the fort of Tumen, and re-established their authority over the neighbouring district. Being soon afterwards reinforced by an additional number of troops, they were enabled to extend their operations, and to erect the fortresses of Tobolsk, Sungur, and Tara. The erection of these and other fortresses was soon attended with a speedy recovery of the whole territory, which Yermac had reduced under the Russian yoke.

This success was only the forerunner of still greater acquisitions. The Russians pushed their conquest far and wide : wherever they appeared, the Tartars were either reduced or exterminated. New towns were built, and colonies were planted on all sides. Before a century had well elapsed, all that vast tract of country, now called Siberia, which stretches from the confines of Europe to the Eastern Ocean, and from the Frozen Sea to

the present frontiers of China, was annexed to
the Russian dominions.

A still larger extent of territory had probably
been won; and all the various tribes of independent Tartary which lie between the southeastern extremity of the Russian empire and
the Chinese wall, would have followed the fate
of the Siberian hordes, if the power of China
had not suddenly interposed.

CHAP. II.

Commencement of hostilities between the Russians and Chinese—disputes concerning the limits of the two empires — treaty of Nershinsk — embassies from the Court of Russia to Pekin — Treaty of Kiachta—establishment of the commerce between the two nations.

TOWARDS the middle of the seventeenth century, the Russians were rapidly extending themselves eastward through that important territory, which lies on each side of the river Amoor.* They soon reduced several independent Tungusian hordes; and built a chain of small fortresses along the banks of the abovementioned river, of which the principal were Albasin, and Kamarskoi Ostrog. Not long afterwards, the Chinese under Camhi† conceived

---

* Amoor is the name given by the Russians to this river; it is called Sakalin-Ula by the Manshurs, and was formerly denominated Karamuran, or the Black River, by the Mongols.

† Camhi was the second emperor of the Manshur race, who made themselves masters of China in 1624.

The Manshurs were originally an obscure tribe of the Tungusian Tartars, whose territories lay South of the Amoor, and

a similar design of subduing the same hordes.
Accordingly, the two great powers of Russia and
China, thus pointing their views to the same
object, unavoidably clashed; and after several
jealousies and intrigues, broke out into open
hostilities about the year 1680. The Chinese
laid siege to Kamarskoi Ostrog, and though
repulsed in this attempt, found means to cut off
several straggling parties of Russians. These
animosities induced the Czar Alexey Michaelo-
vitch to send an embassy to Pekin; but this
measure did not produce the desired effect. The
Chinese attacked Albasin with a considerable
force: having compelled the Russian garrison

---

bordered upon the kingdom of Corea, and the province of
Leaotong. They began to emerge from obscurity at the
beginning of the seventeenth century. About that time their
chief, Aischin-Giord, reduced several neighbouring hordes; and,
having incorporated them with his own tribe, under the general
name of Manshur, he became formidable even to the Chinese.
Shuntschi, grandson of this chief, by an extraordinary concurrence of circumstances, was raised while an infant to the throne
of China, of which his successors still continue in possession.
Shuntschi died in 1662, and was succeeded by Camhi, who is
well known from the accounts of the Jesuit missionaries.

For an account of the revolution of China, see Duhalde,
Descr. de la Chine, Bell's Journey to Pekin.

to capitulate, they demolished that and all the Russian forts upon the Amoor; and returned, with a large number of prisoners, to their own country.

Not long after their departure, a body of sixteen hundred Russians advanced along the Amoor; and constructed a new fort, under the old name of Albasin. The Chinese were no sooner apprised of their return, than they marched instantly towards that river, and sat down before Albasin with an army of seven thousand men, and a large train of artillery. They battered the new fortress for several weeks, without being able to make a breach, and without attempting to take it by storm. The besieged, though not much annoyed by the unskilful operations of the enemy, were exhausted with the complicated miseries of sickness and famine; and notwithstanding they continued to make a gallant resistance, they must soon have sunk under their distresses, if the Chinese had not voluntarily retired, in consequence of a treaty being set afoot between the two courts of

Moscow and Pekin. For this purpose the Russian ambassador Golowin had left Moscow so early as the year 1685, accompanied by a large body of troops, in order to secure his person, and enforce respect to his embassy. The difficulty of procuring subsistence for any considerable number of men in those desolate regions, joined to the ruggedness of the roads, and the length of the march, prevented his arrival at Selenginsk until the year 1687. From thence messengers were immediately dispatched with overtures of peace to the Chinese government at Pekin.

After several delays, occasioned partly by policy, and partly by the posture of affairs in the Tartar country through which the Chinese were to pass, ambassadors left Pekin in the beginning of June, 1689. Golovin had proposed receiving them at Albasin; but while he was proceeding to that fortress, the Chinese ambassadors presented themselves at the gates of Nershinsk, escorted by such a numerous army, and such a formidable train of artillery, that Golovin was

c

constrained, from motives of fear, to conclude the negociation almost upon their own terms.

The conferences were held under tents, in an open plain, near the town of Nershinsk; where the treaty was signed and sealed by the plenipotentaries of the two courts. When it was proposed to ratify it by oath, the Chinese ambassadors offered to swear upon a crucifix; but Golovin preferred their taking an oath in the name of their own Gods.

This treaty first checked the progress of the Russian arms in those parts; and laid the foundations of an important and regular commerce between the two nations.

By the first and second articles, the southeastern boundaries of the Russian empire were formed by a ridge of mountains, stretching north of the Amoor from the sea of Ochotsk to the source of the small river Gorbitza,* then by

---

* There are two Gorbitzas; the first falls into the Amoor, near the conflux of the Argoon and Shilka; the second falls

that river to its influx into the Amoor, and lastly by the Argoon, from its junction with the Shilka up to its source.

By the fifth article, reciprocal liberty of trade was granted to all the subjects of the two empires, who were provided with passports from their respective courts.

This treaty was signed on the 27th of August, in the year 1689, under the reign of Ivan and Peter Alexiewitch, by which the Russians lost, exclusively of a large territory, the navigation of the river Amoor. The importance of this loss was not at that time understood; and has only been felt since the discovery of Kamschatka, and

into the Shilka. The former was meant by the Russians; but the Chinese fixed upon the latter for the boundary, and have carried their point. Accordingly the present limits are somewhat different from those mentioned in the treaty. They are carried from the point, where the Shilka and Argoon unite to form the Amoor, westward along the Shilka, until they reach the mouth of the western Gorbitza; from thence they are continued to the source of the last-mentioned river, and along the chain of mountains as before. By this alteration the Russian limits are somewhat abridged.

of the islands between Asia and America. The
products of these new-discovered countries might,
by means of the Amoor, have been conveyed by
water into the district of Nershinsk, from whence
there is an easy transport by land to Kiachta:
whereas the same merchandise, after being landed
at Ochotsk, is now carried over a large tract of
country, partly upon rivers of difficult navigation,
and partly along rugged and almost impassable
roads.

In return, the Russians obtained what they
long and repeatedly aimed at, a regular and
permanent trade with the Chinese. The first
intercourse between Russia and China commenced in the beginning of the seventeenth
century. At that period a small quantity of
Chinese merchandise was procured, by the merchants of Tomsk and other adjacent towns, from
the Calmucs. The rapid and profitable sale of
these commodities encouraged certain wayvodes
of Siberia to attempt a direct and open communication with China. For this purpose several
deputations were sent at different times to Pekin

from Tobolsk, Tomsk, and other Russian settlements: these deputations, although they failed of obtaining the grant of a regular commerce, were nevertheless attended with some important consequences. The general good reception which the agents met with, tempted the Russian merchants to send occasional traders to Pekin. By these means a faint connection with that metropolis was kept alive: the Chinese learned the advantages of the Russian trade, and were gradually prepared for its subsequent establishment. This commerce, carried on by intervals, was entirely suspended by the hostilities upon the river Amoor. But no sooner was the treaty of Nershinsk signed, than the Russians engaged with extraordinary alacrity in this favourite branch of traffic. The advantages of this trade were soon found to be so considerable, that Peter I. conceived an idea of still farther enlarging it. Accordingly, in 1692, he sent Isbrand Ives, a Dutchman in his service, to Pekin, who requested and obtained, that the liberty of trading to China, which by the late treaty was granted to individuals, should be extended to caravans.

In consequence of this arrangement, successive caravans went from Russia to Pekin, where a caravansary was allotted for their reception; and all their expenses during their continuance in that metropolis defrayed by the Emperor of China. The right of sending these caravans, and the profits resulting from them, belonged to the crown of Russia. In the mean time, private merchants continued as before to carry on a separate trade with the Chinese, not only at Pekin, but also at the head quarters of the Mongols. The camp of these roving Tartars was generally to be found near the conflux of the Orchon and Tola, between the southern frontiers of Siberia and the Mongol desert. A kind of annual fair was held at this spot by the Russian and Chinese merchants, where they brought their respective goods for sale, and continued until they were disposed of. This rendezvous soon became a scene of riot and confusion, and repeated complaints were transmitted to the Chinese Emperor of the drunkenness and misconduct of the Russians. These complaints made a still greater impression from a coincidence of similar excesses, for which the Russians at Pekin had become notorious.

Exasperated by the frequent representations of his subjects, Camhi threatened to expel the Russians from his dominions, and to prohibit them from carrying on any commerce, as well in China as in the country of the Mongols.

These untoward circumstances occasioned another embassy to Pekin, in the year 1719. Leff Vassilievitch Ismailoff, a captain of the Russian guards, who was sent ambassador upon this occasion, succeeded in the negotiation, and adjusted every difficulty to the satisfaction of both parties. At his departure he was permitted to leave behind Laurence Lange, who had accompanied him to Pekin in the character of agent for the caravans, for the purpose of superintending the conduct of the Russians. His residence, however, in that metropolis was but short; for he was soon afterwards compelled by the Chinese to return. His dismission was owing, partly, to a sudden caprice of that suspicious people, and partly to a misunderstanding, which had recently broke out between the two courts, in relation to some Mongol tribes who bordered upon Siberia. A small number of these Mongols had put themselves under the protection of Russia, and were immediately demanded by the Chinese; but the Russians refused compliance, under pretence that no article in the treaty of Nershinsk could, with any appearance of probability, be construed as extending to the Mongols. The Chinese were incensed at this refusal; and their resentment was still further inflamed by the disorderly conduct of the Russian traders, who, freed from all control by the departure of their agent, had indulged, without restraint, their usual propensity to excess. This concurrence of unlucky incidents extorted, in 1722, an order from Camhi for the total expulsion of the Russians from the Chinese and Mongol territories. These orders were rigorously executed; and all intercourse between the two nations immediately ceased.

Affairs continued in this state until the year

1727, when the Count Sava Vladislavitch Ragusinski, a Dalmation, in the service of Russia, was
dispatched to Pekin. His orders were, at all
events, to compose the differences between the
two courts relating to the Mongol tribes; to
settle the southern frontiers of the Russian
empire in that quarter; and to obtain the permission of renewing the trade with China.
Accordingly, that ambassador presented a new
plan for a treaty of limits and commerce to
Yundschin, son and successor of Camhi; by
which the frontiers of the two empires were
finally traced as they exist at present, and the
commerce established upon a permanent basis,
calculated to prevent, as far as possible, all future
sources of misunderstanding. This plan being
approved by the Emperor, Chinese commissioners
were immediately appointed to negotiate with
the Russian ambassador upon the banks of the
Bura, a small river which flows, south of the
confines of Siberia, into the Orchon, near its
junction with the Selenga.

At this conference, the old limits, which are
mentioned in the treaty of Nershinsk, were con-

tinued from the source of the Argoon westwards as far as the mountain Sabyntaban, which is situated at a small distance from the spot where the conflux of the two rivers Uleken and Kemtzak form the Yenisèi: this boundary separates the Russian dominions from the territory of the Mongols, who are under the protection of China.

Is was likewise stipulated, that for the future all negotiations should be transacted between the tribunal of foreign affairs at Pekin, and the board of foreign affairs at St. Petersburg; or in matters of inferior moment, between the commanders of the frontiers.*

The most important articles relating to commerce, were as follow:—

A caravan was allowed to go to Pekin every three years, on condition of its not consisting of

---

* This article was inserted, because the Chinese Emperor, from a ridiculous idea of superiority, had contemptuously refused to hold any correspondence with the court of Russia.

more than two hundred persons; during their residence in that metropolis, their expenses were no longer to be defrayed by the Emperor of China. Notice was to be sent to the Chinese court immediately upon their arrival at the frontiers, where an officer was to meet and accompany them to Pekin.

The privilege before enjoyed by individuals of carrying on a promiscuous traffic in the Chinese and Mongol territories was taken away, and no merchandize belonging to private persons was permitted to be brought for sale beyond the frontiers. For the purpose of preserving, consistently with this regulation, the privilege of commerce to individuals, two places of resort were appointed on the confines of Siberia: one called Kiatchta, from a rivulet of that name near which it stands; and the other Zuruchaitu: at these places a free trade was reciprocally indulged to the subjects of the two nations.

A permission was at the same time obtained for building a Russian church within the pre-

cints of their caravansary; and for the
celebration of divine service, four priests were
allowed to reside at Pekin.* The same favour
was also extended to some Russians scholars†,
for the purpose of learning the Chinese tongue;
in order to qualify themselves for interpreters
between the two nations.

---

* The first Russian Church at Pekin was built for the
accommodation of the Russians taken prisoners at Albasin.
These persons were carried to Pekin, and the place appointed
for their habitation in that city was called the Russian Street, a
name it still retains. They were so well received by the
Chinese, that, upon the conclusion of the treaty of Nershinsk,
they refused to return to their native country. And, as they
intermarried with the Chinese women, their descendants are
quite naturalized; and have, for the most part, adopted not
only the language, but even the religion of the Chinese.
Hence, the above-mentioned church, though it still exists, is
no longer applied to the purpose of divine worship: its priest
was transferred to the Church, which was built within the walls
of the caravansary.

† The good effects of this institution have already been
perceived. A Russian, whose name is Leontieff, after having
resided ten years at Pekin, is returned to Petersburg. He
has given several translations and extracts of some interesting
Chinese publications, viz. Part of the History of China; the
Code of the Chinese Laws; Account of the Towns and
Revenues, &c. of the Chinese Empire, extracted from a
Treatise of Geography, lately printed at Pekin. A short
account of this Extract is given in the Journal of St. Petersburg.

This treaty, called the treaty of Kiachta, was, on the fourteenth of June, 1728, concluded and ratified by the Count Ragusinski and three Chinese plenipotentaries upon the spot, where Kiachta was afterwards built: it is the basis of all transactions since carried on between Russia and China.

One innovation in the mode of carrying on the trade to China, which has been introduced since the accession of the present Empress, Catherine II. deserves to be mentioned in this place. Since the year 1755 no caravans have been sent to Pekin. Their first discontinuance was owing to a misunderstanding between the two courts of Petersburg and Pekin, in 1759. Their disuse, after the reconciliation had taken place, arose from the following circumstances. The exportation and importation of many principal commodities, particularly the most valuable furs, were formerly prohibited to individuals, and solely appropriated to caravans belonging to the crown. By these restrictions the Russian trade to China was greatly shackled and circumscribed. The Empress (who, amidst many excellent regulations which characterise her reign, has shewn herself invariably attentive to the improvement of the Russian commerce) abolished, in 1762, the monopoly of the fur trade, and renounced in favour of her subjects the exclusive privilege which the crown enjoyed of sending caravans to Pekin. By these concessions the profits of the trade have been considerably increased: the great expense, hazard, and delay, of transporting the merchandize occasionally from the frontiers of Siberia to Pekin, has been retrenched; and Kiachta is now rendered the centre of the Russian and Chinese commerce.

CHAP. III.

Account of the Russian and Chinese settlements upon the confines of Siberia—description of the Russian frontier town Kiachta—of the Chinese frontier town Maitmatschin —its buildings, pagodas, &c.

By the last-mentioned treaty it was stipulated, that the commerce between Russia and China should be transacted at the frontiers. Accordingly two spots were marked out for that purpose upon the confines of Siberia, where they border upon the Mongol desert; one near the brook Kiachta, and the other at Zuruchaitu, The description of the former of these places forms the subject of this chapter.

This settlement consists of a Russian and Chinese town, both situated in a romantic valley, surrounded by high, rocky, and for the most part, well-wooded mountains. This valley is intersected by the brook Kiachta, which rises in Siberia, and, after washing both the Russian and

Chinese town, falls into the Bura, at a small distance from the frontiers.

The Russian settlement is called Kiachta, from the above-mentioned brook: it lies in 124 degrees, 18 minutes longitude from the isle of Fero, and 35 degrees north latitude, at the distance of 5514 versts from Moscow, and 1532 from Pekin.

It consists of a fortress, and a small suburb. The fortress, which is built upon a gentle rise, is a square enclosed with palisadoes, and strengthened with wooden bastions at the several angles. There are three gates, at which guards are constantly stationed: one of the gates faces the north, a second the south towards the Chinese frontiers, and a third the east close to the brook Kiachta. The principal public buildings in the fortress are a wooden church, the governor's house, the custom house, the magazine for provisions, and the guard house. It contains also a range of shops and warehouses, barracks for the garrison, and several houses longing to the crown; the latter are generally inhabited by the principal merchants. These buildings are mostly of wood.

The suburb, which is surrounded with a wooden wall covered at the top with chevaux-de-frise, contains no more than a hundred and twenty houses, very irregularly built; it has the same number of gates as the fortress, which are also guarded. Without this suburb, upon the high road leading to Selenginsk, stand a few houses, and the magazine for rhubarb.

This settlement is but indifferently provided with water, both in quality and quantity; for although the brook Kiachta is dammed up as it flows by the fortress, yet it is so shallow in summer, that, unless after heavy rains, it is scarcely sufficient to supply the inhabitants. Its stream is troubled and unwholesome, and the springs which rise in the neighbourhood are either foul or brackish: from these circumstances, the principal inhabitants are obliged to send for water from a spring in the Chinese district.

The soil of the adjacent country is mostly sand or rock, and extremely barren. If the frontiers of Russia were extended about nine versts more south to the rivulet of Bura, the inhabitants of Kiachta would then enjoy good water, a fruitful soil, and plenty of fish, all which advantages are at present confined to the Chinese.

The garrison of Kiachta consists of a company of regular soldiers, and a certain number of Cossacks; the former are occasionally changed, but the latter are fixed inhabitants of the place. It is the province of the commander to inspect the frontiers, and, in conjunction with the president of the Chinese merchants, to settle all affairs of an inferior nature; but in matters of importance recourse must be had to the chancery of Selenginsk, and to the governor of Irkutsk. The Russian merchants, and the agents of the Russian trading company, are the principal inhabitants of Kiachta.

The limits westwards from this settlement to the river Selenga, and eastwards as far as Tchi-

koi, are bounded with chevaux-de-frise, placed
there to prevent a contraband trade in cattle, for
the exportation of which a considerable duty is
paid to the crown. All the outposts along the
frontiers, westwards as far as the government of
Tobolsk, and eastwards to the mountains of
snow, are under the command of the governor
of Kiachta.

The most elevated of the mountains that sur-
round the valley of Kiachta, and which is
called by the Mongols, Burgultei, commands
the Russian as well as the Chinese town; for
this reason, the Chinese, at the conclusion of the
last frontier treaty, demanded the cession of
this mountain, under the pretext that some of
their deified ancestors were buried upon its
summit. The Russians gave way to their re-
quest, and suffered the boundary to be brought
back to the north side of the mountain.

The Chinese town is called, by the Chinese
and Mongols, Maimatschin, which signifies for-

tress of commerce. The Russians term it the
Chinese Village (Kitaiskaia Sloboda) and also
Naimatschin, which is a corruption of Maimatschin.   It is situated about a hundred and
forty yards south of the fortress of Kiachta,
and nearly parallel to it.   Midway between this
place and the Russian fortress, two posts about
ten feet high are planted, in order to mark the
frontier of the two empires: one is inscribed
with Russian, the other with Manshur cha-
racters.*

Mainatschin has no other fortification than a
wooden wall, and a small ditch of about three
feet broad ; the latter was dug in the year 1756;
during the war between the Chinese and the
Calmucs. The town is of an oblong form; its
length is seven hundred yards, and its breadth
four hundred.   On each of the four sides a
large gate faces the principal streets ; over each

* Upon the mountain to the west of Kiachta, the limit is
again marked ; on the Russian side by a heap of stones and
earth, ornamented on the top with a cross, and on the Chinese
by a pile of stones in the shape of a pyramid.

of these gates there is a wooden guard house
for the Chinese garrison, which consists of Mongols in tattered clothes, and armed with clubs.
Without the gate, which looks to the Russian
frontiers, and about the distance of eight yards
from the entrance, the Chinese have raised a
wooden screen, so constructed as to intercept all
view of the streets from without.

This town contains two hundred houses and
about twelve hundred inhabitants. It has two
principal streets of about eight yards broad,
crossing each other in the middle at right
angles, with two by-streets running from north
to south. They are not paved, but are laid
with gravel, and kept remarkably clean.

The houses are spacious, uniformly built of
wood, of only one story, not more than fourteen
feet high, plastered and whitewashed; they
are constructed round a court yard of about
seventy feet square, which is strewed with gravel, and has an appearance of neatness. Each
house consists of a sitting room, some ware-

houses, and a kitchen. In the houses of the wealthier sort the roof is made of plank; but in meaner habitations, of lath, covered over with turf. Towards the streets most of the houses have arcades of wood, projecting forwards from the roof like a penthouse, and supported by strong pillars. The windows are large, after the European manner, but on account of the dearness of glass and Russian talc, are generally of paper, excepting a few panes of glass in the sitting room.

The sitting room looks seldom towards the streets: it is a kind of shop, where the several patterns of merchandize are placed in recesses, fitted up with shelves, and secured with paper doors for the purpose of keeping out the dust. The windows are generally ornamented with little paintings, and the walls are hung with Chinese paper. Half the floor is of hard beaten clay; the other half is covered with boards, and rises about two feet in height. Here the family sit in the day time and sleep at night. By the side of this raised part, and nearly upon the same level, there is a square brick stove, with a straight perpendicular cylindrical excavation, which is heated with small pieces of wood. From the bottom of this stove a tube descends, and is carried zigzag under the boarded floor above mentioned, and from thence to a chimney which opens into the street. By this contrivance, although the stove is always open and the flame visible, yet the room is never troubled in the least degree with smoke. There is scarcely any furniture in the room, excepting one large dining table in the lower part, and two small lackered ones upon the raised floor: one of these tables is always provided with a chafing dish, which serves to light their pipes when the stove is not heated.

In this room there are several small niches covered with silken curtains, before which are placed lamps that are lighted upon festivals; these niches contain painted paper idols, a stone or metal vessel, wherein the ashes of incense are collected, several small ornaments and artificial flowers: the Chinese readily allow strangers to draw aside the curtains, and look at the idols.

The Bucharian* merchants inhabit the south-west quarter of Maimatschin. Their houses are not so large nor commodious as those of the Chinese, although the greatest part of them carry on a very considerable commerce.

The Surgutschéi, or governor of Maimatschin, has the care of the police, as well as the direction of all affairs relating to commerce: he is generally a person of rank, oftentimes a Mandarin, who has misbehaved himself in another station, and is sent here as a kind of punishment. He is distinguished from the rest by the crystal button of his cap, and by a peacock's feather† hanging behind. The

---

* " The chief merchandizes which the Bucharians bring to Russia, are cotton, stuffs, and half silks, spun and raw cotton, lamb skins, precious stones, gold dust, unprepared nitre, sal-ammoniac, &c." See Russia, or a complete Historical Account of all the nations that compose that empire, vol. ii. p. 141, a very curious and interesting work lately published.

† In china the princes of the blood wear three peacock's feathers, nobles of the highest distinction two, and the lower class of the nobility one. It is also a mark of high rank to drive a carriage with four wheels. The governor of Maimatschin rode in one with only two wheels. All the Chinese wear buttons of different colours in their caps, which also denote the rank.

Chinese give him the title of Amban, which signifies commander-in-chief; and no one appears before him without bending the knee, in which posture the person who brings a petition must remain until he receives the governor's answer. His salary is not large; but the presents which he receives from the merchants amount annually to a considerable sum.

The most remarkable public buildings in Maimatschin are, the governor's house, the theatre, and two pagodas.

The governor's house is larger than the others, and better furnished; it is distinguished by a chamber where the court of justice is held, and by two high poles before the entrance ornamented with flags.

The theatre is situated close to the wall of the town near the great pagoda; it is a kind of small shed, neatly painted, open in front, and merely spacious enough to contain the stage; the audience stand in the street. Near it are

two high poles, upon which large flags with
Chinese inscriptions are hoisted on festivals.
On such occasions the servants belonging to
the merchants play short burlesque farces in
honour of their idols.

The smallest of the two pagodas is a wooden
building, standing upon pillars, in the centre
of the town, at the place where the two principal
streets cross.   It is a Chinese tower of two
stories, adorned on the outside with small
columns, paintings, and little iron bells, &c.
The first story is square, the second octangular.
In the lower story is a picture representing the
god Tien, which signifies, according to the
explanation of the most intelligent Chinese, the
most high god, who rules over the thirty-two
heavens.   The Manshurs, it is said, call this
idol Abcho; and the Mongols, Tingheru heaven,
or the god of heaven.   He is represented
sitting with his head uncovered, and encircled
with a ray* of glory, similar to that which

* When Mr. Pallas obtained permission of the governor to
see this temple, the latter assured him that the Jesuits of Pekin

surrounds the head of our Saviour in the Roman Catholic paintings; his hair is long and flowing; he holds in his right hand a drawn sword, and his left is extended as in the act of giving a benediction. On one side of this figure two youths, on the other a maiden and a grey-headed old man, are delineated.

The upper story contains the picture of another idol in a black and white chequered cap, with the same figures of three young persons and a little old man. There are no altars in this temple, and no other ornaments excepting these pictures and their frames. It is opened only on festivals, and strangers cannot see it without permission.

The great pagoda, situated before the governor's house, and near the principal gate,

---

and their converts adored this idol. From whence he ingeniously conjectures, either that the resemblance between this idol, and the representations of our Saviour by the Roman Catholics, was the occasion of this assertion; or that the Jesuits, in order to excite the devotion of the converts, have, out of policy, given to the picture of our Saviour a resemblance to the Tien of the Chinese.

looking to the south, is larger and more
magnificent than the former.   Strangers are
allowed to see it at all times, without the least
difficulty, provided they are accompanied by one
of the priests, who are always to be found in the
area of the temple.   This area is surrounded
with chevaux-de-frise: the entrance is from
the south, through two gates, with a small
building between them.   In the inside of this
building are two recesses with rails before them,
behind which the images of two horses as large
as life are coarsely moulded out of clay ; they are
saddled and bridled, and attended by two
human figures dressed like grooms: the horse
to the right is of a chesnut colour, the other is
dun, with a black mane and tail; the former is in
the attitude of springing, the latter of walking.
Near each horse a banner of yellow silk, painted
with silver dragons, is displayed.

In the middle of this area are two wooden
turrets surrounded with galleries; a large bell
of cast iron, which is struck occasionally with a
large wooden mallet, hangs in the eastern

turret; the other contains two kettle drums of
an enormous size, similar to those made use of
in the religious ceremonies of the Calmucs.　On
each side of this area are ranges of buildings,
inhabited by the priest of the temple.

This area communicates by means of a hand-
some gateway with the inner court, which is
bordered on each side by small compartments
open in front, with rails before them; in the
inside of these compartments the legendary
stories of the idols are exhibited in a series of
historical paintings.　At the farther extremity
of this court stands a large building, constructed
in the same style of architecture as the temple.
The inside is sixty feet long, and thirty broad;
it is stored with ancient weapons, and instruments of war of a prodigious size, such as spears,
scythes, and long pikes, with broad blades,
shields, coats of arms, and military ensigns,
representing hands,* dragons' heads, and other
carved figures.　All these warlike instruments

* These hands resemble the manipulary standards of the Romans.

are richly gilded, and ranged in order upon
scaffolds along the wall.   Opposite the entrance
a large yellow standard, embroidered with foliage
and silver dragons, is erected; under it, upon a
kind of altar, there is a series of little oblong
tables, bearing Chinese inscriptions.

An open gallery, adorned on both sides with
flower-pots, leads from the back door of the
armoury to the colonnade of the temple.   In
this colonnade two slate tablets are placed, in
wooden frames, about six feet high and two
broad, with long inscriptions relating to the
building of the temple.   Before one of these
plates a small idol of a hideous form stands
upon the ground, enclosed in a wooden case.

The temple itself is an elegant Chinese building, richly decorated on the outside with columns
lackered, and gilded carved work, small bells,
and other ornaments peculiar to the Chinese
architecture.   Within there is a rich profusion
of gilding, which corresponds with the gaudiness
of the exterior.   The walls are covered thick

with paintings, exhibiting the most celebrated exploits of the principal idol.

This temple contains five idols of a colossal stature, sitting cross-legged upon pedestals in three recesses, which fill the whole northern side.

The principal idol is seated alone, in the middle recess, between two columns, entwined with gilded dragons. Large streamers of silk, hanging from the roof of the temple, veil in some measure the upper part of the image. His name is Ghedsur, or Ghessur Chan;* the Chinese call him Loo-ye, or the first and most ancient; and the Manshurs, Guanlöe, or the superior god. He is of a gigantic size, surpassing more than four-fold the human stature,

---

* The Mongols and Calmucs call him by this name of Ghessur Chan; and although they do not reckon him among their divinities, yet they consider him as a great hero, the Bacchus and Hercules of Eastern Tartary, who was born at the source of the Choango, and who vanquished many monsters. They have in their language a very long history of his heroical deeds. His title, in the Mongol tongue, is as follows: Arban Zeeghi Essin Ghessur Bogdo Chan; the king of the ten points of the compass, or the monarch Ghessur Chan.

with a face glistening like burnished gold, black hair and beard. He wears a crown upon his head, and is richly dressed in the Chinese fashion: his garments are not moulded out of clay, as those of the other idols; but are made of the finest silk. He holds in his hands a kind of tablet, which he seems to read with deep attention. Two small female figures, resembling girls of about fourteen years of age, stand on each side of the idol, upon the same pedestal; one of which grasps a roll of paper. At the right-hand of the idol lie seven golden arrows, and at his left a bow.

Before the idol is a spacious enclosure, surrounded with rails, within which stands an altar with four colossal figures, intended probably to represent the principal mandarins of the deified Ghessur. Two of these figures are dressed like judges, and hold before them small tablets, similar to that in the hands of the principal idol. The two other figures are accoutred in complete armour; one wears a turban, and carries, upon the left shoulder, a large sword sheathed, with the hilt upwards. The other has a hideous copper-coloured face, a large belly, and grasps in his right hand a lance with a broad blade.

Although all the remaining idols in the temple are of an enormous size, yet they are greatly surpassed in magnitude by Ghessur Chan.

The first idol in the recess to the right is called Maooang, or the Otschibanni of the Mongols. He has three ghastly copper-coloured faces, and six arms; two of his arms brandish two sabres crossways over the head; a third bears a looking glass, and a fourth a kind of square, which resembles a piece of ivory. The two remaining arms are employed in drawing a bow, with an arrow laid upon it, ready to be discharged. This idol has a mirror upon his breast, and an eye in his navel: near it are placed two small figures; one holds an arrow, and the other a little animal.

The next idol in the same recess is called by the Chinese Tsaudsing, or the gold and silver

E

god; and by the Mongols Tsagan-Dsambala.
He wears a black cap, and is dressed, after the
Chinese fashion, in sumptuous robes of state;
he bears in his hand a small jewel casket. Near
him also stand two little figures, one of which
holds a truncated branch.

In the recess to the left is the God Chusho,
called by the Manshurs Chua-schan, and by the
Mongols Galdi, or the Fire God. He is represented with a frightful fiery reddish face; clad
in complete armour he wields a sword half
drawn out of the scabbard, and seems on the
point of starting up from his seat. He is
attended by two little halbadiers, one of whom
is crying; and the other bears a fowl upon his
hand, which resembles a sea-pheasant.

The other idol in the same recess is the god
of oxen, Niu-o. He appears to be sitting in a
composed posture; he is habited like a Mandarin, and is distinguished by a crown upon
his head. He has, in common with the other
idols, a mirror upon his breast. The Chinese

imagine him to be the same with the Yamandaga
of the Mongols; and it is said his Manshurish
name is Chain Killova; his Mongol name,
which relates to the history of Ghessur, is Bars-
Batir, the Hero of Tygers.

Before these several idols there are tables, or
altars, on which cakes, pastry, dried fruit, and
flesh, are placed, on festival and prayer days; on
particular occasions even whole carcases of sheep
are offered up. Tapers and lamps are kept
burning day and night before the idols. Among
the utensils of the temple, the most remarkable
is a vessel shaped like a quiver, and filled with
flat pieces of cleft reed, on which short Chinese
devices are inscribed. These devices are taken
out by the Chinese on new-year's day, and are
considered as oracles, which foretel the good or
ill luck of the person, by whom they are drawn,
for the following year. There lies also upon a
table a hollow wooden black lackered helmet,
which all persons of devotion strike with a
wooden hammer, whenever they enter the
temple. This helmet is regarded with such

peculiar awe, that no strangers are permitted to
handle it, although they are allowed to touch
even the idols themselves.

The first day of the new and full moon is
appointed for the celebration of worship.   Upon
each of those days no Chinese ever fails to make
his appearance once in the temple; he enters
without taking off his cap*, joins his hands
before his face, bows five times to each idol,
touches with his forehead the pedestal on which
the idol sits, and then retires.   Their principal festivals are held in the first month of their year,
which answers to February.   It is called by them,
as well as by the Mongols, the white month; and
is considered as a lucky time for the transaction
of business; at that time they hoist flags before
the temples; and place meat upon the tables of
the idols, which the priests take away in the
evening, and eat in the small apartments of the
interior court.   On these solemnities plays are

---

* They do not take off their caps out of respect; for among
the Chinese, as well as other Eastern nations, it is reckoned a
mark of disrespect to uncover the head before a superior.

performed in the theatre, in honour of the idols:
the pieces are generally satirical, and mostly
written against unjust magistrates and judges.

But although the Chinese have such few
ceremonies in their system of religious worship,
yet they are remarkably infected with superstition.   Mr. Pallas gives the following description
of their behaviour at Maimatschin during an
eclipse of the moon.   At the close of the evening
in which the eclipse appeared, all the inhabitants
were indefatigable in raising an incessant uproar,
some by hideous shrieks, others by knocking
wood and beating cauldrons; the din was height-
ened by striking the bell and beating the kettle
drums of the great pagoda.   The Chinese sup-
pose, that during an eclipse the wicked spirit of
the air, called by the Mongols Arachulla, is
attacking the moon; and that he is frightened
away by these hideous shrieks and noises.
Another instance of superstition fell under the
observation of Mr. Pallas while he was at Maimatschin.   A fire broke out in that town with
such violence that several houses were in flames

None of the inhabitants, however, attempted to extinguish it; they stood indeed in idle consternation round the fire; and some of them sprinkled occasionally water among the flames, in order to sooth the fire god, who, as they imagined, had chosen their houses as a sacrifice. Indeed if the Russians had not exerted themselves in quenching the fire, the whole place would probably have been reduced to ashes*.

---

* This account of Kiachta and Maimatschin is taken from Mr. Pallas's description of Kiachta, in the journal of his travels through Siberia. Every circumstance relating to the religious worship of the Eastern nations is in itself so interesting, that I thought it would not be unacceptable to my readers to give a translation of the above passages respecting the Chinese pagodas and idols: although in a work treating of the new discoveries, and the commerce which is connected with them. In the above-mentioned journal the ingenious author continues to describe, from his own observations, the manners, customs, dress, diet, and several other particulars relative to the Chinese; which, although exceedingly curious and interesting, are foreign to my present purpose, and would have been incompatible with the size of the present work.

No writer has placed the religion and history of the Tartar nations in a more explicit point of view than Mr. Pallas; every page in his interesting journal affords striking proofs of this assertion. He has lately thrown new lights upon this obscure subject, in a recent publication concerning the Tartars, who inhabit parts of Siberia, and the territory which lies between that country and the Chinese wall. Of this excellent work the first volume appeared in 1776, and contains the genealogy, history, laws, manners, and customs, of this extraordinary people, as they are divided into Calmucs, Mongols, and Burats. The second volume describes, with minuteness and accuracy, the tenets and religious ceremonies which distinguish the votaries of Shamanism from the followers of Dalai-Lama, the two great sects into which these tribes are distinguished.

CHAP. IV.

Commerce between the Chinese and Russians—list of the principal exports and imports—duties—average amount of the Russian trade.

THE merchants of Maimatschin come from the northern provinces of China, chiefly from Pekin, Nankin, Sandchue, and other principal towns. They are not settled at this place with their wives and families: for it is a remarkable circumstance, that there is not one woman in Maimatschin. This restriction arises from the policy of the Chinese government, which totally prohibits the women from having the slightest intercource with foreigners. No Chinese merchant engages in the trade to Siberia who has not a partner. These persons mutually relieve each other. One remains for a stated time, usually a year, at Kiachta; and when his partner arrives with a fresh cargo of Chinese merchandize, he then returns home with the Russian commodities.

Most of the Chinese merchants understand the Mongol tongue, in which language, commercial affairs are generally transacted. Some few indeed speak broken Russian, but their pronunciation is so soft and delicate, that it is difficult to comprehend them. They are not able to pronounce the R, but instead of it make use of an L; and when two consonants come together, which frequently occurs in the Russian tongue, they divide them by the interposition of a vowel. This failure in articulating the Russian language seems peculiar to the Chinese, and is not observable in the Calmucs, Mongols, and other neighbouring nations.

The commerce between the Russians and Chinese is entirely a trade of barter, that is, an exchange of one merchandize for another. The Russians are prohibited to export their own coin, nor indeed could the Chinese receive it, even should that prohibition be taken off; for no specie is current among them except bullion.*

* The Chinese have no gold or silver coin. These metals are always paid in bullion; and for the purpose of ascertaining the

And the Russians find it more advantageous to
take merchandize in exchange, than to receive
bullion at the Chinese standard.   The common
method of transacting business is as follows.
The Chinese merchant comes first to Kiachta,
and examines the merchandize he has occasion
for in the warehouse of the Russian trader; he
then goes to the house of the latter, and adjusts

---

weight, every Chinese merchant is constantly provided with a
pair of scales.   As gold is very scarce in China, silver is the
great vehicle of commerce.   When several authors affirm that
the Russians draw large quantities of silver from China,
they mistake an accidental occurrence for a general and standing
fact   During the war between the Chinese and Calmucs, the
former had occasion to purchase at Kiachta, provision, horses,
and camels, for which they paid silver.   This traffic brought
such a profusion of that metal into Siberia, that its price was
greatly reduced below its real value.   A pound of silver was,
at that period, occasionally sold at the frontiers for eight or
nine roubles, which at present fetches fifteen or sixteen.   But
since the conclusion of these wars, by the total reduction of the
Calmucs under the Chinese yoke, Russia receives a very small
quantity of silver from the Chinese.

   The silver imported to Kiachta is chiefly brought by the
Bucharian merchants, who sell cattle to the Chinese in exchange
for that metal, which they afterwards dispose of to the Russians
for European manufactures.   Gold-dust is also occasionally
obtained from the same merchants ; the quantity however of
those metals procured at Kiachta is so inconsiderable, as scarcely
to deserve mention.   The whole sum imported to Kiachta, in
1777, amounted to only 18,215 roubles.

the price over a dish of tea. Both parties next
return to the magazine, and the goods in question are there carefully sealed in the presence of
the Chinese merchant. When this ceremony is
over they both repair to Maimatschin; the
Russian chooses the commodities he wants, not
forgetting to guard against fraud by a strict
inspection. He then takes the precaution to
leave behind a person of confidence, who remains
in the warehouse until the Russian goods are
delivered, when he returns to Kiachta with the
Chinese merchandize.

The principal commodities which Russia
exports to China are as follow:

FURS AND PELTRY.

It would be uninteresting to enumerate all
the furs and skins brought for sale to Kiachta,
which form the most important article of exportation on the side of the Russians. The
most valuable of these furs are the skins of
sea-otters, beavers, foxes, wolves, bears, Bucharian lambs, Astrachan sheep, martens, sables,
ermines, and grey squirrels

The greatest part of these furs and skins are drawn from Siberia and the New Discovered Islands: this supply, however, is not alone fully adequate to the demand of the market at Kiachta. Foreign furs are therefore imported to St. Petersburg, and from thence sent to the frontiers. England alone furnishes a large quantity of beaver and other skins, which she draws from Hudson's Bay and Canada.

CLOTH.

Cloth forms the second article of exportation which Russia exports to China.

The coarse sort is manufactured in Russia; the finer sort is foreign, chiefly English, Prussian, and French.

An arshire of foreign cloth fetches, according to its fineness, from two to four roubles.

Camlets.

Calimancoes.

Druggets.

White flannels, both Russian and foreign.

The remaining articles are,

Rich stuffs.

Velvets.

Coarse linen, chiefly manufactured in Russia.

Russia leather.

Tanned hides.

Glass ware and looking glasses.

Hardware, namely, knives, scissors, locks, &c.

Tin.

Russian talc.

Cattle, chiefly camels, horses, and horned cattle.

The Chinese also pay very dear for hounds, grey-hounds, barbets, and dogs for hunting wild boars.

Provisions.

Meal.—The Chinese no longer import such large quantities of meal as formerly, since they have employed the Mongols to cultivate the lands lying near the river Orchon, &c. &c.

List of the most valuable commodities
procured from China.

RAW AND MANUFACTURED SILK.

The exportation of raw silk is prohibited in China under pain of death: large quantities however are smuggled every year into Kiachta, but not sufficient to answer the demands of the Russian merchants.

A pood of the best sort is estimated at one hundred and fifty roubles; of the worst sort at seventy-five.

The manufactured silks are of various sorts, fashions, and prices, viz. satins, taffaties, dammasks, and gauzes, skeins of silk died of all colours, ribbands, &c. &c.

RAW AND MANUFACTURED COTTON.

Raw cotton is imported in very large quantities; a great part of this commodity is employed in packing up the china ware, and by these means is conveyed into the inland part of Russia without any additional expense of carriage.

A pood sells for — from 4 roubles, 8o. cop to 12.

Of the manufactured cotton, that which the Russians called Kitaika, and the English Nankeen, has the most rapid sale. It is the most durable, and, in proportion to its goodness, the cheapest of all the Chinese stuffs; it is stained red, brown, green, and black.

Teas.

The teas which are brought into Russia are much superior in flavour and quality to those which are sent to Europe from Canton. The original goodness of the teas is probably the same in both cases; but it is conjectured, that the transport by sea considerably impairs the aromatic flavour of the plant. This commodity, now become so favourite an object of European luxury, is esteemed by the Russian merchants the most profitable article of importation.

At Kiachta a pound of the best
tea* is estimated at . . . . . 2 roubles.
Common ditto at . . . . . . 1 „
Inferior at . . . . 40 copecs.

---

* At Petersburg, a pound of the best green tea fetches three roubles.

PORCELAIN OF ALL SORTS.

For some years past the Chinese have brought to Kiachta parcels of porcelain, painted with European figures, with copies of several favorite prints and images of the Grecian and Roman deities.

Furniture, particularly Japan cabinets and cases, lackered and varnished tables and chairs, boxes inlaid with mother-of-pearl, &c. &c.

Fans, toys, and other small wares.

Artificial flowers.

Tiger and panther skins.

Rubies,* but neither in large quantities nor of great value.

White lead, vermillion, and other colours.

Canes.

Tobacco.

Rice.

Sugar Candy.

---

* Rubies are generally procured by smuggling ; and by the same means pearls are occasionally disposed of to the Chinese, at a very dear rate. Pearls are much sought for by the Chinese ; and might be made a very profitable article.

Preserved ginger, and other sweet-meats.

Rhubarb.

Musk.

It is very difficult to procure the genuine Thibet musk, because the Chinese purchase a bad sort, which comes from Siberia, with which they adulterate that which is brought from Thibet.

Russia draws great advantages from the Chinese trade. By this traffic, its natural productions, and particularly its furs and skins, are disposed of in a very profitable manner. Many of these furs procured from the most easterly parts of Siberia, are of such little value that they would not answer the expense of carriage into Russia; while the richer furs, which are sold to the Chinese at a very high price, would, on account of their dearness, seldom meet with purchasers in the Russian dominions. In exchange for these commodities the Russians receive from China several valuable articles of commerce, which they would otherwise be obliged to buy at a much dearer rate

F

from the European powers, to the great disadvantage of the balance of their trade.

I have before observed, that formerly the exportation and importation of the most valuable goods were prohibited to individuals; at present only the following articles are prohibited. Among the exports, fire-arms and artillery; gunpowder and ball; gold and silver, coined and uncoined; stallions and mares; skins of deer, rein-deer, elks, and horses; beavers' hair, potash, rosin, thread, and tinsel lace:* among the imports, salt, brandy, poisons, copper-money, and rhubarb.

The duties paid by the Russian merchants are very considerable; great part of the merchandize is taxed at 25 per cent.

Furs, cattle, and provisions, pay a duty of 23 per cent.

Russian manufactures, 18 per cent.

---

* Tinsel lace is smuggled to the Chinese with considerable profit, for they pay nearly as much for it as if it was solid silver.

One per cent. is also deducted from the price of all goods for the expense of deepening the river Selenga; and 7 per cent. for the support of the custom-house.

Some articles, both of export and import, pay no duty. The exported are, writing, royal, and post paper, Russia cloth of all sorts and colours, excepting peasants cloth. The imported are, satins, raw and stained cottons, porcelain, earthenware, glass corals, beads, fans, all musical instruments, furniture, lackered and enamelled ornaments, needles, white lead, rice, preserved ginger, and other sweet-meats.

The importance of this trade will appear from the following table:—

Table of exportation and importation at Kiachta this year.

	ROUBLES.	COP.
Custom-house duties	481,460.	59$\frac{1}{2}$
Importation of Chinese goods to the value of	1,466,497.	3$\frac{3}{4}$
Of gold and silver	11,215.	
Total of importation	1,484,712.	3$\frac{3}{4}$

	ROUBLES.	COP.
Exportation of Russian commodities	1,313,621.	35.
From this table it appears, that the total sum of export and import amounts to	2,868,333.	

In this calculation, however, the contraband trade is not included, which is very large ; and as this year was not so favourable to this traffic as the preceding ones, we may venture to estimate the gross amount of the average trade to China at near 4,000,000 roubles.

CHAP. V.

Description of Zuruchaitu—and its trade—Transport of the merchandize through Siberia.

THE general account of the Russian commerce to China has been given in the preceding chapter, because almost the whole traffic is confined to Kiachta. The description of Zuruchaitu, which was also fixed by the treaty of Kiachta for the purpose of carrying on the same trade, will be comprised, of course, in a narrow compass.

Zuruchaitu is situated in 137° longitude, and 49°. 20 N. latitude, upon the western branch of the river Argoon, at a small distance from its source. It is provided with a small garrison, and a few wretched barracks, surrounded with chevaux-de-frise. No merchants are settled at this place; they come every summer from Nershinsk, and other Russian towns, in order to meet two parties of Mongol troops : these troops are sent from the Chinese towns Naun and Merghen, and arrive at the frontiers about July. They encamp near Zuruchaitu upon the other side of the river Argoon, and barter with the Siberian merchants a few Chinese commodities, which they bring with them.

Formerly the commerce carried on at Zuruchaitu was more considerable; but at present it is so trifling, that it hardly deserves to be mentioned. These Mongols furnish the district of Nershinsk with bad tea and tobacco, bad silks, and some tolerable cottons. They receive in return ordinary furs, cloth, cattle, and Russian leather. This trade lasts about a month or six weeks, and the annual duties of the customs amount upon an average to no more than 500 roubles. About the middle of August the Mongols retire; part proceed immediately to China, and the others descend the stream of the Amoor as far as its mouth, in order to observe if there has been no usurpation upon the limits. At the same time the Russian merchants return to

Nershinsk, and, were it not for the small garrison, Zuruchaitu would remain uninhabited.

The Russian commodities are transported by land from Petersburg and Moscow to Tobolsk. From thence the merchants may embark upon the Irtish down to its junction with the Oby; then they either tow up their boats, or sail up the last-mentioned river as far as Marym, where they enter the Ket, which they ascend to Makoffskoi Ostrog. At that place the merchandize is carried about ninety versts by land to the Yenisèi. The merchants then ascend that river, the Tunguska, and Angara, to Irkutsk, cross the lake Baikal, and go up the river Selenga almost to Kiachta.

It is a work of such difficulty to ascend the streams of so many rapid rivers, that this navigation eastwards can hardly be finished in one summer;* for which reason the merchants com-

---

* Some of these rivers are only navigable in spring, when the snow water is melting; in winter, the rivers are in general frozen.

monly prefer the way by land. Their general rendezvous is the fair of Irbit near Tobolsk; from thence they go in sledges during winter to Kiachta, where they arrive about February, the season in which the chief commerce is carried on with the Chinese. They buy in their route all the furs they find in the small towns, where they are brought from the adjacent countries, When the merchants return in spring with the Chinese goods, which are of greater bulk and weight than the Russian commodities, they proceed by water; they then descend the streams of most of the rivers, namely, the Selenga, Angara, Tunguska, Ket, and Oby, to its junction with the Irtish; they ascend that river to Tobolsk, and continue by land to Moscow and Petersburg.

Before the passage from Ochotsk to Bolcheresk was discovered in 1716, the only communication between Kamtchatka and Siberia was by land; the road lay by Anadirsk to Yakutsk. The furs*

* The furs, which are generally landed upon the eastern coast of Kamtchatka, are either sent by sea to Bolcheresk, or

of Kamtchatka and of the eastern isles are now conveyed from that peninsula by water to Ochotsk; from thence to Yakutsk by land on horseback, or by rein-deer; the roads are so very bad, lying either through a rugged mountainous country, or through marshy forests, that the journey lasts at least six weeks. Yakutsk is situated upon the Lena, and is the principal town, where the choicest furs are brought in their way to Kiachta, as well from Kamtchatka as from the northern parts of Siberia, which lay upon the rivers Lena, Yana, and Endigirka. At Yakutsk the goods are embarked upon the Lena, towed up the stream of that river as far as Vercholensk, or still farther to Katsheg; from thence they are transported over a short tract of land to the rivulet Buguldeika, down that stream to the lake Baikal, across that lake to the mouth of the Selenga, and up that river to the neighbourhood of Kiachta.

---

are transported across the Peninsula in sledges drawn by dogs. The latter conveyance is only used in winter; it is the usual mode of travelling in that country. In summer there is no conveyance, as the Peninsula contains neither oxen, horses, or rein-deer.

In order to give the reader some notion of that vast tract of country, over which the merchandize is frequently transported by land carriage, a list of the distances is here subjoined.

From Petersburg to Moscow .	734	versts.
Moscow to Tobolsk . .	2385	"
Tobolsk to Irkutsk . .	2918	"
Irkutsk to Kiachto . .	471	"
	6508	
From Irbit to Tobolsk . . .	420	"
From Irkutsk to Nershinsk .	1129	"
Nershinsk to Zuruchaitu	370	"
From Ochotsk to Yakutsk . .	927	"
Yakutsk to Irkutsk . .	2433	"
From Selenginsk to Zuruchaitu	850	"
Zuruchaitu to Pekin . .	1588	"
Kiachta to Pekin . .	1532	"

The Chinese transport their goods to Kiachta chiefly upon camels. It is four or five days journey from Pekin to the wall of China, and forty-six from thence across the Mongol desert to Kiachta.

CHAP. VI.

Tartarian rhubard brought to Kiachta by the Bucharian merchants—method of examining and purchasing the roots —different species of rheum which yield the finest rhubarb — price of rhubarb in Russia—exportation—superiority of the Tartarian over the Indian rhubarb.

Europe is supplied with rhubarb from Russia and the East Indies. The former is generally known by the name of Turkey rhubarb, because we used to import it from the Levant in our commerce with the Turks, who procured it through Persia from the Bucharians. And it still retains its original name, although instead of being carried, as before, to Constantinople, it is now brought to Kiachta by the Bucharian merchants, and there disposed of to the Russians. This appellation is indeed the most general; but it is mentioned occasionally by several authors, under the different denominations of Russian, Tartarian, Bucharian, and Thibet rhubarb. This sort is exported from Russia in large roundish pieces, freed from the bark, with a hole through the middle; they are externally of a yellow colour, and when cut appear variegated with lively reddish streaks.

The other sort is called by the druggists Indian rhubarb, and is procured from Canton in longer, harder, heavier, and more compact pieces, than the former; it is more astringent, and has somewhat less of an aromatic flavour; but, on account of its cheapness, is more generally used than the Tartarian or Turkey rhubarb.

The government of Russia has reserved to itself the exclusive privilege of purchasing rhubarb; it is brought to Kiachta by some Bucharian merchants, who have entered into a contract to supply the crown with that drug in exchange for furs. These merchants come from the town of Selin, which lies south-westward of the Koko-Nor, or Blue Lake, towards Thibet. Selin, and all the towns of Little Bucharia, viz. Kashkar, Yerken, Atrar, &c. are subject to China.

The best rhubarb purchased at Kiachta is produced upon a chain of rocks, which are very high, and for the most part destitute of wood; they lie north of Selin, and stretch as far as the Koko-Nor. The good roots are distinguished by large and thick stems. The Tanguts, who are employed in digging up the roots, enter upon that business in April or May. As fast as they take them out of the earth, they cleanse them from the soil, and hang them upon the neighbouring trees to dry, where they remain until a sufficient quantity is procured; after which they are delivered to the Bucharian merchants. The roots are wrapped up in woollen sacks, carefully preserved from the least humidity, and are in this manner transported to Kiachta upon camels.

The exportation of the best rhubarb is prohibited by the Chinese, under the severest penalties. It is procured, however, in sufficient quantities, sometimes by clandestinely mixing it with inferior roots, and sometimes by means of a contraband trade. The College of Commerce at Petersburg is solely empowered to receive this drug, and appoints agents at Kiachta for that purpose. Much care is taken in the choice; for it is examined, in the presence of the Bucharian merchants, by an apothecary, commissioned by government, and resident at Kiachta. All the worm-eaten roots are rejected; the remainder are bored through, in order to ascertain their soundness, and all the parts which appear in the least damaged or decayed are cut away. By these means even the best roots are diminished a sixth part, and the refuse is burnt, in order to prevent its being brought another year.*

Linnæus has distinguished the different species of rhubarb by the names of Rheum Palmatum, R. Rhaponticum, R. Rhabarbarum, R. Compactum, and R. Ribes.

---

* When Mr. Pallas was at Kiachta, the Bucharian merchant, who supplies the crown with rhubarb, brought some pieces of white rhubarb, which had a sweet taste, and was equal in its effects to the best sort.

Botanists have long differed in their opinions, which of these several species is the true rhubarb; and that question does not appear to be as yet satisfactorily cleared up.   However, according to the notion which is most generally received, it is supposed to be the Rheum Palmatum; the seeds of which were originally procured from a Bucharian merchant, and distributed to the principal botanists of Europe.   Hence this plant has been cultivated with great success; and is now very common in all our botanical gardens. The learned Doctor Hope, professor of medicine and botany in the University of Edinburgh, having made trials of the powder of this root, in the same doses in which the foreign rhubarb is given, found no difference in its effects; and from thence conclusions have been drawn with great appearance of probability, that this is the plant which produces the true rhubarb.   But this inference does not appear to be absolutely conclusive; for the same trials have been re-peated, and with similar success, upon the roots, of the R. Rhaponticum and R. Rhabarbarum.

The leaves of the R. Rhaponticum are round, and sometimes broader than they are long. This species is found abundantly in the loamy and dry deserts between the Volga and the Yaik,* towards the Caspian Sea. It was probably from this sort that the name Rha, which is the Tartarian appellation of the river Volga, was first applied by the Arabian physicians to the several species of rheum. The roots, however, which grow in these warm plains are rather too astringent; and therefore ought not to be used in cases where opening medicines are required. The Calmucs call it Badshona, or a stomachic. The young shoots of this plant, which appear in March or April, are deemed a good anti-scorbutic; and are used as such by the Russians. The R. Rhaponticum is not to be found to the west of the Volga. The seeds of this species produced at Petersburg plants of a much greater size than the wild ones: the leaves were large, and of a roundish cordated figure.

---

* The Yaik falls into the Caspian Sea, about four degrees to the east of the Volga.

The R. Rhabarbarum grows in the crevices of bare rocky mountains, and also upon gravelly soils: it is more particularly found in the high vallies of the romantic country situated beyond Lake Baikal. Its buds do not shoot before the end of April; and it continues in flower during the whole month of May. The stalks of the leaves are eaten raw by the Tartars: they produce upon most persons, who are unaccustomed to them, a kind of spasmodic contraction of the throat, which goes off in a few hours; it returns, however, at every meal, until they become habituated to this kind of diet. The Russians make use of the leaves in their hodge-podge: accordingly, soups of this sort affect strangers in the manner above mentioned. In Siberia the stalk is sometimes preserved as a sweet-meat; and a custom prevails among the Germans of introducing at their tables the buds of this plant, as well as of the Rheum Palmatum, instead of cauliflower.

The R. Rhaponticum which commonly grows near the torrents has, as well as the R. Rhabarbarum of Siberia, the upper part of its roots commonly rotten, from too much moisture: accordingly, a very small portion of the lower extremity is fit for use. The Russian College of Physicians order, for the use of their military hospitals, large quantities of these roots to be dug up in Siberia, which are prescribed under the name of Rhapontic. But the persons employed in digging and preparing it are so ill instructed for that purpose, that its best juices are frequently lost. These roots ought to be drawn up in spring, soon after the melting of the snows, when the plant retains all its sap and strength; whereas they are not taken out of the ground before August, when they are wasted by the increase of the stem, and the expansion of the leaves. Add to this, that the roots are no sooner taken up, than they are immediately sliced in small pieces, and thus dried; by which means the medicinal qualities are sensibly impaired.

For the same roots, which in this instance were of such little efficacy, when dried with proper precaution, have been found to yield a very excellent rhubarb. The process observed for this purpose, by the ingenious Mr. Pallas, was as follows:—The roots, immediately after being drawn out, were suspended over a stove, where being gradually dried, they were cleansed from the earth; by these means, although they were actually taken up in autumn, they so nearly resembled the best Tartarian rhubarb in colour, texture, and purgative qualities, that they answered in every respect the same medicinal purposes.

A German apothecary, named Zuchert, made similar trials with the same success, both on the Rheum Rhabarbarum and R. Rhaponticum, which grow in great perfection on the mountains in the neighbourhood of Nershinsk. He formed plantations of these herbs on the declivity of a rock,* covered with one foot of good

---

* In order to succeed fully in the plantation of rhubarb, and to procure sound and dry roots, a dry, light soil with a rocky foundation, where the moisture easily filters off, is essentiall necessary.

mould, mixed with an equal quantity of sand and gravel. If the summer proved dry, the plants were left in the ground; but if the season was rainy, after drawing out the roots, he left them for some time in the shade to dry, and then replanted them. By this method of cultivation he produced in seven or eight years very large and sound roots, which the rock had prevented from penetrating too deep; and when they were properly dried, one scruple was as efficacious as half a drachm of Tartarian rhubarb.

From the foregoing observations it follows, that there are other plants, besides the Rheum Palmatum, the roots whereof have been found to be similar both in their appearance and effects, to what is called the best rhubarb, And indeed, upon enquiries made at Kiachta concerning the form and leaves of the plant which produces that drug, it seems not to be the R. Palmatum, but a species with roundish scolloped leaves, and most probably the R. Rhaponticum; for Mr. Pallas, when he was at Kiachta, applied for information to a Bucharian merchant of Selin-Chotton, who now supplies the Crown with rhubarb; and his description of that plant answered to the figure of the Rheum Rhaponticum. The truth of this description was still further confirmed by some Mongol travellers who had been in the neighbourhood of the Kokor-Nor and Thibet, and had observed the rhubarb growing wild upon those mountains.

The experiments also made by Zuchert and others, upon the roots of the R. Rhabarbarum and R. Rhaponticum, sufficiently prove, that this valuable drug was procured from those roots in great perfection. But as the seeds of the Rheum Palmatum were received from the father of the above-mentioned Bucharian merchant, as taken from the plant which furnishes the true rhubarb, we have reason to conjecture, that these three species, viz. R. Palmatum, R. Rhaponticum, and R. Rhabarbarum, when found in a dryer and milder Alpine climate, and in proper situations, are indiscriminately drawn up; whenever the size of the plant seems to promise a fine root. And perhaps the remarkable difference of the rhubarb,

imported to Kiachta, is occasioned by this indis-
criminate method of collecting them. Most
certain it is, that these plants grow wild upon the
mountains, without the least cultivation; and
those are esteemed the best which are found
near the Koko-Nor, and about the sources of the
river Koango.

Formerly the exportation of rhubarb was confined to the Crown of Russia; and no persons
but those employed by government, were allowed
the permission of sending it to foreign countries;
this monopoly, however, has been taken off,
and the free exportation of it from St. Petersburg granted to all persons upon paying the
duty. It is sold in the first instance by the
College of Commerce, for the profit of the
Sovereign, and is preserved in their magazines
at St. Petersburg. The current price is settled
every year by the College of Commerce.

It is received from the Bucharian merchants at
Kiachta, in exchange for furs; and the prime
cost is rated at 16 roubles per pood. By adding

the pay of the commisioners who purchase it, and of the apothecary who examines it, and allowing for other necessary expenses, the value of a pood at Kiachta amounts to 25 roubles; add to this the carriage from the frontiers to St. Petersburg, and it is calculated that the price of a pood stands the Crown at 30 roubles. The largest exportation of rhubarb ever known from Russia, was made in the year 1765, when 1350 poods were exported, at 65 roubles per pood.

EXPORTATION OF RHUBARB
FROM ST. PETERSBURG.

In 1777, 29 poods 13 pounds, at 76¼ Dutch* dollars, or 91 roubles 30 copecs per pood.

In 1778, 23 poods 7 pounds, at 80 ditto, or 96 roubles.

In 1778, 1055 poods were brought by the Bucharian merchants to Kiachta; of which 680 poods 19 pounds were selected. The interior

* If we reckon a Dutch dollar, upon an average, to be worth 1 rouble 20 copecs.

consumption of the whole empire of Russia, for 1777, amounted to only 6 poods 5 pounds.*

The superiority of this Tartarian rhubarb, over that procured from Canton, arises probably from the following circumstances :—

1. The southern parts of China are not so proper for the growth of this plant as the mountains of Little Bucharia.

2. There is not so exact an examination made in receiving it from the Chinese at Canton, as from the Bucharians at Kiachta. For the merchants, who purchase this drug at Canton, are obliged to accept it in the gross, without separating the bad roots, and cutting away the decayed parts, as is done at Kiachta.

3. It is also probable, that the long transport of this drug by sea is detrimental to it, from the humidity which it must necessarily contract during so long a voyage.

* This calculation comprehends only the rhubarb purchased at the different magazines belonging to the College of Commerce ; for what was procured by contraband is of course not included.

CHAP. VII.

For the convenience of the Reader, the following table exhibits in one point of view the longitude and latitude of the principal places mentioned in this performance. Their longitudes are estimated from the first meridian of the Isle of Fero, and from that of the Royal Observatory at Greenwich. The longitude of Greenwich from Fero is computed at 17° 34′ 45′′. The longitude of the places marked * has been taken from astronomical observations.

| | Latitude. | | | Longitude. | | | | |
| | | | | Fero. | | | Greenwich. | |
	D.	M.	S.	D.	M.	S	D.	M.
*Petersburg	59	56	23	48	0	0	30	25†
*Moscow	55	45	45	55	6	30	37	31
*Archangel	64	33	24	56	15	0	38	40
*Tobolsk	58	12	22	85	40	0	68	26
*Tomsk	56	30	0	102	50	0	85	15
*Irkutsk	52	18	15	122	13	0	104	38
*Selenginsk	51	6	0	124	18	30	106	44
Kiachta	35	0	0	124	18	0	106	43
*Yakutsk	62	1	50	147	0	0	129	25
*Ochotsk	59	22	0	160	7	0	142	32
*Bolcheresk	52	55	0	174	13	0	156	38
*Port of St. Peter and Paul	53	1	0	176	10	0	158	36
Eastern extremity of Siberia . .	66	0	0	200	0	0	182	25
Unalashka — According to the general Map of Russia	58	0	0	223	0	0	205	25
Unalashka — According to the chart of Krenitzin & Levasheff	53	30	0	205	30	0	187	55

† I have omitted the seconds in the longitude from Greenwich.

PRELIMINARY OBSERVATIONS

CONCERNING

KAMTCHATKA, &c.

WHERE THE FURS ARE COLLECTED FOR THE CHINESE MARKET.

CHAP. VIII.

Discovery and conquest of Kamtchatka—state of that peninsula—population—tribute—productions, &c.

THE peninsula of Kamtchatka was not discovered by the Russians before the latter end of the last century. The first expedition towards those parts was made in 1696, by sixteen Cossacks, under the command of Lucas Semænoff Morosko, who was sent against the Koriacks of the river Opooka by Volodimer Atlassoff, commander of Anadirsk. Morosko continued his march until he came within four days' journey of the river Kamtchatka, and having rendered a Kamtchadal village tributary, he returned to Anadirsk.

The following year Atlassoff himself, at the head of a larger body of troops, penetrated into the peninsula, took possession of the river Kamtchatka by erecting a cross upon its banks; and built some huts upon the spot, where Upper Kamtchatkoi Ostrog now stands.

These expeditions were continued during the following years: Upper and Lower Kamtchatkoi Ostrogs and Bolcheresk were built; the southern district conquered and colonized; and in 1711, the whole peninsula was finally reduced under the dominion of the Russians.

During some years the possession of Kamtchatka brought very little advantage to the Crown, excepting the small tribute of furs exacted from the inhabitants. The Russians, indeed, occasionally hunted in that peninsula foxes, wolves, ermines, sables, and other animals, whose valuable skins form an extensive article of commerce among the eastern nations. But the fur trade carried on from thence was inconsiderable, until the Russians discovered the islands situated between Asia and America, in a series of voyages. Since these discoveries, the variety of rich furs, which are procured from those islands, has greatly increased the trade of Kamtchatka, and rendered it a very important branch of the Russian commerce.

The peninsula of Kamtchatka lies between 51 and 62 degrees of north latitude, and 173 and 182 of longitude from the Isle of Fero. It is bounded on the east and south by the sea of Kamtchatka, on the west by the seas of Ochotsk and Penshinsk, and on the north by the country of the Koriacks.

It is divided into four districts, Bolcheresk, Tigilskaia Krepost, Verchnei or Upper Kam-tchatkoi Ostrog, and Nishnei or Lower Kam-tchatkoi Ostrog. The government is vested in the chancery of Bolcheresk, which depends upon, and is subject to, the inspection of the chancery of Ochotsk. The whole Russian force stationed in the peninsula consists of no more than three hundred men.

The present population of Kamtchatka is very small, amounting to scarce four thousand souls. Formerly the inhabitants were more numerous, but in 1768, that country was greatly depopulated by the ravages of the small-pox, by which disorder five thousand, three hundred, and sixty-eight persons were carried off. There are now only seven hundred and six males in the whole peninsula who are tributary, and a hundred and fourteen in the Kuril Isles, which are subject to Russia.

The fixed annual tribute consists in 279 sables, 464 red foxes, 50 sea-otters with a dam, and 38 cub sea-otters. All furs exported from Kamtchatka pay a duty of ten per cent. to the Crown; the tenth of the cargoes brought from the New Discovered Islands is also delivered into the customs.

Many traces of volcanos have been observed in this peninsula; and there are some mountains, which at present are in a burning state. The most considerable of these volcanos is situated near the Lower Ostrog. In 1762, a great noise was heard issuing from the inside of that mountain, and flames of fire were seen to burst from different parts. These flames were immediately succeeded by a large stream of melted snow water, which flowed into the neighbouring valley, and drowned two Kamtchadals, who were at that time upon a hunting party. The ashes, and other combustible matter, thrown from the mountain, spread to the circumference of three hundred versts. In 1767, there was another discharge, but less considerable. Every night flames of fire were observed streaming from the mountain; and the eruption which attended them, did no small damage to the inhabitants of the Lower Ostrog. Since that year no flames have been seen; but the mountain emits a constant smoke. The same phænomenon is also observed upon another mountain, called Tabaetshinskian.

The face of the country throughout the peninsula is chiefly mountainous. It produces in some parts birch, poplars, alders, willows, underwood, and berries of different sorts.   Greens and other vegetables are raised with great facility ; such as white   cabbage,   turnips,   radishes,   beet-root, carrots, and some cucumbers.   Agriculture is in a very low state, which is chiefly owing to the nature of the soil and the severe hoar frosts ; for though some trials have been made with respect to the cultivation of corn and oats, barley, and rye have been sown ; yet no crop has ever been procured sufficient in quantity or quality to answer the pains and expense of raising it. Hemp, however, has of late years been cultivated with great success.*

Every year a vessel belonging to the Crown, sails from Ochotsk to Kamtchatka laden with salt, provisions, corn, and Russian manufactures ; and returns in June or July of the following year with skins and furs for the Chinese market.

---

* Journal of St. Petersburg.

CHAP. IX.

SINCE the conclusion of Beering's voyage, which was made at the expense of the Crown, the prosecution of the new discoveries began by him has been almost entirely carried on by individuals. These persons were principally merchants of Irkutsk, Yakutsk, and other natives of Siberia, who formed themselves into small trading companies, and fitted out vessels at their joint expense.

Most of the vessels which are equipped for these expeditions are two masted: they are commonly built without iron, and in general so badly constructed, that it is wonderful how they can weather so stormy a sea. They are called in Russian, Skitiki, or sewed vessels, because the planks are sewed together with thongs of leather. Some few are built in the river of Kamtchatka; but they are for the most part constructed at the haven of Ochotsk. The largest of these vessels are manned with seventy men, and the smallest with forty. The crew generally consists of an equal number of Russians and Kamtchadals. The latter occasion a considerable saving, as their pay is small; they also resist, more easily than the former, the attacks of the scurvy. But Russian mariners are more enterprising and more to be depended upon in time of danger than the others; some, therefore, are unavoidably necessary.

The expenses of building and fitting out the vessels are very considerable; for their is nothing at Ochotsk but timber for their construction. Accordingly cordage sails, and some provisions, must be brought from Yakutsk upon horses. The dearness of corn and flour, which must be transported from the districts, lying about the river Lena, renders it impossible to lay in any large quantity for the subsistence of the crew during a voyage, which commonly lasts three or four years. For this reason, no more is provided than is necessary to supply the Russian mariners with quass and other fermented liquors.

From the excessive scarcity of cattle, both at Ochotsk, and Kamtchatka very little provision is laid in at either of those places: but the crew provide themselves with a large store of the flesh of sea animals, which are caught and cured upon Beering's Island, where the vessels for the most part winter.

After all expenses are paid, the equipment of each vessel ordinarily costs from 15,000 to 20,000 roubles; and sometimes the expenses amount to 30,000. Every vessel is divided into a certain number of shares, generally from thirty to fifty; and each share is worth from 300 to 500 roubles.

The risk of the trade is very great, as ship-wrecks are common in the sea of Kamtchatka,

which is full of rocks and very tempestuous.
Besides, the crews are frequently surprised and
killed by the islanders, and the vessels destroyed.
In return, the profits arising from these voyages
are very considerable, and compensate the in-
conveniences and dangers attending them. For,
if a ship comes back after having made a profitable voyage, the gain, at the most moderate
computation, amounts to cent. per cent., and
frequently to as much more. Should the vessel
be capable of performing a second expedition,
the expenses, are, of course, considerably lessened,
and the shares are at a lower price.

Some notion of the general profits arising
from this trade (when the voyage is successful),
may be deduced from the sale of a rich cargo
of furs, brought to Kamtchatka, from the New-
Discovered Islands, in a vessel belonging to
Ivan Popoff.

The tenth part of the skins being delivered to
the customs, the remainder was distributed in
fifty-five shares. Each share consisted of twenty

sea-otters, sixteen black and brown foxes, ten red foxes, three sea-otter tails; and such a portion was sold upon the spot from 800 to 1000 roubles: so that, according to this price, the whole lading was worth about 50,000 roubles.

CHAP. X.

THE principal furs and skins procured from the peninsula of Kamtchatka and the New Discovered Islands are sea-otters, foxes, sables, ermines, wolves, bears, &c. These furs are transported to Ochotsk by sea, and from thence carried to Kiachta upon the frontiers of Siberia, where the greatest part of them are sold to the Chinese at a very considerable profit.

Of all these furs the skins of the sea-otters are the richest and most valuable. Those animals resort in great numbers to the Aleütian and Fox Islands; they are called by the Russians Bobry Morski or sea-beavers, and sometimes Kamtchadal beavers, on account of the resemblance of their fur to that of the common beaver. From these circumstances several authors have been led into a mistake, and have supposed that this animal is of the beaver species, whereas it is the true sea-otter.

The females are called Matka or dams; and the cubs, till five months old, Madviedki or little bears, because their coat resembles that of a bear; they lose that coat after five months, and then are called Koschloki.

The fur of the finest sort is thick and long, of a dark colour, and a fine glossy hue. They are taken four ways; struck with darts as they are sleeping upon their backs in the sea, followed in boats and hunted down till they are tired, surprised in caverns, and taken in nets.

Their skins fetch different prices, according to their quality.

	ROUBLES.	ROUBLES.
At Kamtchatka the best sell for per skin from	30	to 40
Middle sort	20	to 30
Worst sort	15	to 25

	ROUBLES.	ROUBLES.
At Kiachta the old and middle-aged sea-otter skins are sold to the Chinese per skin from	80 to	100
The worst sort	30 to	40

As these furs fetch so great a price to the Chinese, they are seldom brought into Russia for sale: and several, which have been carried to Moscow as a tribute, were purchased for 30 roubles per skin; and sent from thence to the Chinese frontiers, where they were disposed of at a very high interest.

There are several species of foxes, whose skins are sent from Kamtchatka into Siberia and Russia. Of these the principal are the black foxes, the Petsi or Arctic foxes, and the red and stone foxes.

The finest black foxes are caught in different parts of Siberia, and more commonly in the northern regions between the rivers Lena, Indigirka, and Kovyma: the black foxes found upon the remotest eastern islands discovered by the

Russians, or the Lyssie Ostrova, are not so valuable. They are very black and large ; but the coat for the most part is as coarse as that of a wolf. The great difference in the fineness of the fur, between these foxes and those of Siberia arises probably from the following circumstances :—In those islands the cold is not so severe as in Siberia ; and as there is no wood, the foxes live in holes and caverns of the rocks ; whereas in the above-mentioned parts of Siberia, there are large tracts of forests in which they find shelter. Some black foxes, however, are occasionally caught in the remotest eastern islands, not wholly destitute of wood, and these are of great value. In general the Chinese, who pay the dearest for black furs, do not give more for the black foxes of the New Discovered Islands than from 20 to 30 roubles per skin.

The Arctic or ice foxes are very common upon some of the New Discovered Islands. They are called Petsi by the Russians, and by the Germans blue foxes. Their natural colour is of a bluish grey or ash colour; but they change

their coat at different ages, and in different
seasons of the year. In general they are born
brown, are white in winter, and brown in summer; and in spring and autumn, as the hair
gradually falls off, the coat is marked with
different specks and crosses.

	ROUBLES.	COP.
At Kiachta all the several varieties sell upon an average to the Chinese per skin from 50 copecs to	$2\frac{2}{3}$	
Stone foxes at Kamtchatka per skin from	1 to $2\frac{1}{2}$	
Red Foxes, from 80 copecs to .	1	80
At Kiachta, from 80 copecs to .	9	
Common wolves' skins at per skin	2	
Best sort per skin from . . .	8 to 16	
Sables per ditto	$2\frac{1}{2}$ to 10	

A pood of the best sea-horse teeth sells

	ROUBLES.
At Yakutsk for	10
Of the middling	8
Inferior ditto	5 to 7

Four, five, or six teeth generally weigh a pood.
and sometimes, but very rarely, three. They are
sold to the Chinese, Mongols, and Calmucks.

CHAP. XI.

Commencement and progress of the first Russian discoveries in the sea of Kamtchatka—general division of the New Discovered Islands, where furs were procured for the China market.

A THIRST after riches was the chief motive which excited the Spaniards to the discovery of America; and which turned the attention of other maritime nations to that quarter. The same passion for riches occasioned, about the middle of the sixteenth century, the discovery and conquest of Northern Asia, a country, before that time, as unknown to the Europeans as Thule to the ancients. The first foundation of this conquest was laid by the celebrated Yermac, at the head of a band of adventurers, less civilized, but, at the same time, not so inhuman as the conquerors of America. By the accession of this vast territory, now known by the name of Siberia, the Russians have acquired an extent of empire never before attained by any other nation.

The first project* for making discoveries in
that tempestuous sea, which lies between Kamtchatka and America, was conceived and planned
by Peter I., the greatest sovereign who ever
sat upon the Russian throne. The nature and
completion of this project under his immediate
successors are well known to the public from
the relation of the celebrated Muller. No
sooner had Beering† and Tschirikoff, in the

---

* There seems a want of connection in this place, which will
be cleared up by considering, that, by the conquest of Siberia,
the Russians advanced to the shores of the Eastern Ocean, the
scene of the discoveries here alluded to.

† Beering had already made several expeditions in the sea
of Kamtchatka, by orders of the Crown, before he undertook
the voyage mentioned in the text.

In 1728, he departed from the mouth of the Kamtchatka
river, in company with Tschirikoff. The purport of this voyage
was to ascertain, whether the two continents of Asia and America
were separated; and Peter I. a short time before his death, had
drawn up instructions with his own hand for that purpose.
Beering coasted the eastern shore of Siberia as high as latitude
67° 18′; but made no discovery of the opposite continent.

In 1729, he set sail again for the prosecution of the same
design; but this second attempt equally failed of success.

In 1741, Beering and Tschirikoff went out upon the celebrated expedition (alluded to in the text, and which is so often
mentioned in the course of this work) towards the coasts of
America. This expedition led the way to all the important discoveries since made by the Russians.

Beering's vessel was wrecked in December of the same year;
and Tschirikoff landed at Kamtchatka on the 9th October, 1742.

prosecution of this plan, opened their way to islands abounding in valuable furs, than private merchants immediately engaged with ardour in similar expeditions; and, within a period of ten years, more important discoveries were made by these individuals, at their own private cost, than had been hitherto effected by all the expensive efforts of the Crown.

Soon after the return of Beering's crew from the island where he was shipwrecked and died, and which is called after his name, the inhabitants of Kamtchatka ventured over to that island, to which the sea-otters and other sea-animals were accustomed to resort in great numbers. Mednoi Ostroff Island, which lies full in sight of Beering's Isle, was an easy and speedy discovery.

These two small uninhabited spots were for some time the only islands that were known; until a scarcity of land and sea-animals, whose numbers were greatly diminished by the Russian hunters, occasioned other expeditions.

Several of the vessels which were sent out upon these voyages were driven by stormy weather to the south-east; and discovered by that means the Aleütian Isles, situated about the 195th* degree of longitude, and but moderately peopled.

From the year 1745, when it seems these islands were first visited, until 1750, when the first tribute of furs was brought from thence to Ochotsk, the government appears not to have been fully informed of their discovery. In the last-mentioned year, one Lebedeff was commander of Kamtchatka. From 1755 to 1760, Captain Tsheredoff and Lieutenant Kashkareff were his successors. In 1760, Feodor Ivanovitch Soimonoff, governor of Tobolsk, turned his attention to the above-mentioned islands; and, the same year, Captain Rtistsheff, at Ochotsk, instructed Lieutenant Shmaleff, the

---

* The author reckons, throughout this narrative, the longitude from the first meridian of the Isle of Fero. The longitude and latitude, which he gives to the Fox Islands, corresponds exactly with those in which they are laid down upon the general map of Russia. The longitude of Beering's and of the Aleütian Isles, are somewhat different.

same who was afterwards commander in Kamtchatka, to promote and favour all expeditions in those seas. Until this time, all the discoveries subsequent to Beering's voyage were made, without the interposition of the court, by private merchants in small vessels fitted out at their own expense.

As to the New Discovered Islands, no credit must be given to a chart published in the Geographical Calendar of St. Petersburg for 1774; in which they are inaccurately laid down. Nor is the ancient chart of the new discoveries, published by the Imperial Academy, and which seems to have been drawn up from mere reports, more deserving of attention.

The late navigators give a far different description of the Northern Archipelago. From their accounts we learn, that Beering's Island is situated due east from Kamtchatkoi Noss, in the 185th degree of longitude. Near it is another island; and, at some distance from them, east-south-east, there are three small islands, named by their inhabitants, Attack, Semitshi, and Shemiya; these are properly the Aleütian Isles; they stretch from west-north-west towards east-south-east, in the same direction as Beering's Islands, in the longitude of 195, and latitude 54.

To the north-east of these, at the distance of 600 or 800 versts, lies another group of six or more islands, known by the name of the Andrea-noffskie Ostrova.

South-east, or east-south-east, of these, at the distance of about 15 degrees, and north by east of the Aleütian, begins the chain of Lyssie Ostrova, or Fox Islands: this chain of rocks and isles stretches east-north-east between the 56 and 61 degrees of north latitude, from 211 degrees of longitude most probably to the Continent of America; and in a line of direction, which crosses with that in which the Aleütian Isles lie. The largest and most remarkable of these islands are Umnak, Aghunalashka, or, as it is commonly shortened, Unalashka, Kadyak, and Alagshak.

Of these and the Aleütian Isles, the distance and position are tolerably well ascertained by ships' reckonings, and latitudes taken by pilots. But the situation of the Andreanoffskie Isles* is still somewhat doubtful, though probably their direction is east and west; and some of them may unite with that part of the Fox Islands which are most contiguous to the opposite continent.

A very full and judicious account of all the discoveries hitherto made in the Eastern Ocean has been published by the celebrated Mr. Muller†. Meanwhile, I hope the following account, extracted from the original papers, and procured from the best intelligence, will be the more acceptable to the public; as it may

---

* These are the same islands which are called, by Mr. Stæhlin, Anadirsky Islands, from their supposed vicinity to the river Anadyr.

† Mr. Muller has already arranged and put in order several of the journals, and sent them to the Board of Admiralty at St. Petersburg, where they are at present kept, together with the charts of the respective voyages.

prove an inducement to the Russians to publish fuller and more circumstantial relations. Besides, the reader will find here a narrative more authentic and accurate, than what has been published in the above-mentioned work; and several mistakes in that memoir are here corrected.

CHAP. XIII.

Voyages in 1745, *from Kamtchatka—first discovery of the Aleütian Isles by Michael Nevodtsikoff.*

A voyage made in the year 1745 by Emilian Bassoff is scarce worth mentioning, as he only reached Beering's Island, and two smaller ones, which lie south of the former, and returned on the 31st of July, 1746.

The first voyage which is in any wise re-markable, was undertaken in the year 1745. The vessel was a Shitik named Eudokia, fitted out at the expense of Aphanassei Tsebaefskoi, Jacob Tsiuproff and others; she sailed from the Kamtchatka river Sept. 19, under the command of Michael Nevodtsikoff a native of Tobolsk. Having discovered three unknown islands, they wintered upon one of them, in order to kill sea-otters, of which there was a large quantity. These islands were undoubtedly the nearest

Aleütian Islands:* the language of the inhabitants was not understood by an interpreter, whom they had brought with them from Kamtchatka. For the purpose therefore of learning this language, they carried back with them one of the islanders; and presented him to the chancery of Bolcheresk, with a false account of their proceedings. This islander was examined as soon as he had acquired a slight knowledge of the Russian language; and as it is said, gave the following report. He was called Temnac, and Att was the name of the island of which he was a native. At some distance from thence lies a great island called Sabya, of which the inhabitants, are denominated Rogii: these inhabitants, as the Russians understood, or thought they understood him, made crosses, had books, and fire-arms, and navigated in baidars or leathern canoes. At no great distance from the island where they wintered, there were two

---

* The small group of islands lying S.E. of Beering's Island, are the real Aleütian Isles; they are sometimes called the Nearest Aleütian Islands, and the Fox Islands, the Furthest Aleütian Isles.

well-inhabited islands: the first lying east-south-east and south-east by south, the second east and east by south. The above-mentioned islander was baptized under the name of Paul, and sent to Ochotsk.

As the misconduct of the ship's crew towards the natives was suspected, partly from the loss of several men, and partly from the report of those Russians, who were not concerned in the disorderly conduct of their companions, a strict examination took place; by which the following circumstances relating to the voyage were brought to light.

According to the account of some of the crew, and particularly of the commander, after six days' sailing they came in sight of the first island on the 24th of September, at mid-day. They sailed by, and towards evening they discovered the second island, where they lay at anchor until the next morning.

The 25th several inhabitants appeared on the coast, and the pilot was making towards shore in the small boat, with an intention of landing; but observing their numbers increase to about a hundred, he was afraid of venturing among them, although they beckoned to him. He contented himself, therefore, with flinging some needles amongst them: the islanders in return threw into the boat some sea-fowl of the cormorant kind. He endeavoured to hold a conversation with them by means of the interpreters, but no one could understand their language. And now the crew endeavoured to row the vessel out to sea; but the wind being contrary, they were driven to the other side of the same island, where they cast anchor.

The 26th, Tsiuproff having landed with some of the crew in order to look for water, met several inhabitants: he gave them some tobacco and small Chinese pipes; and received in return a present of a stick, upon which the head of a seal was carved. They endeavoured to wrest his hunting gun from him; but upon his refusing to part with it and retiring to the small boat, the islanders ran after him, and seized the rope by which the boat was made fast to shore. This violent attack obliged Tsiuproff to fire; and having wounded one person in the hand, they all let go their hold; and he rowed off to the ship. The savages no sooner saw that their companion was hurt, than they threw off their clothes, carried the wounded person naked into the sea, and washed him. In consequence of this encounter the ship's crew would not venture to winter at this place, but rowed back again to the other island, where they came to an anchor.

The next morning Tsiuproff, and a certain Shaffyrin landed with a more considerable party: they observed several traces of inhabitants; but meeting no one, they returned to the ship, and coasted along the island. The following day the Cossack Shekurdin went on shore, accompanied by five sailors: two of whom he sent back with a supply of water; and remained himself with the others in order to hunt sea-otters. At night they came to some dwellings inhabited by five families: upon their approach

the natives abandoned their huts with precipi-
tation, and hid themselves among the rocks.
Shekurdin no sooner returned to the ship, than
he was again sent on shore with a larger company, in order to look out for a proper place to
lay up the vessel during winter. In their way
they observed fifteen islanders upon an height;
and threw them some fragments of dried fish,
in order to entice them to approach nearer.
But as this overture did not succeed, Tsiuproff,
who was one of the party, ordered some of the
crew to mount the height, and to seize one of
the inhabitants, for the purpose of learning
their language : this order was accordingly executed, notwithstanding the resistance which the
islanders made with their bone spears; the
Russians immediately returned with their
prisoner to the ship. They were soon afterwards
driven to sea by a violent storm, and beat
about from the 2nd to the 9th of October, during
which time they lost their anchor and boat;
at length they came back to the same island,
where they passed the winter.

Soon after their landing they found in an adjacent hut the dead bodies of two of the inhabitants, who had probably been killed in the last encounter. In their way the Russians were met by an old woman, who had been taken prisoner and set at liberty. She was accompanied by thirty-four islanders of both sexes, who all came dancing to the sound of a drum; and brought with them a present of coloured earth. Pieces of cloth, thimbles, and needles, were distributed among them in return; and they parted amicably. Before the end of October, the same persons, together with the old woman and several children, returned dancing as before, and brought birds, fish, and other provision. Having passed the night with the Russians, they took their leave. Soon after their departure, Tsiuproff, Shaffyrin, and Nevodsikoff, accompanied by seven of the crew, went after them, and found them among the rocks. In this interview the natives behaved in the most friendly manner, and exchanged a baidar and some skins for two shirts. They were observed to have hatchets of sharpened stone, and needles made of bone: they lived on the flesh of sea-otters, seals, and sea-lions, which they killed with clubs and bone lances.

So early as the 24th of October, Tsiuproff had sent ten persons, under the command of Larion Belayeff, upon a reconnoitering party. The latter treated the inhabitants in a hostile manner, upon which they defended themselves as well as they could with their bone lances. This resistance gave him a pretext for firing; and accordingly he shot the whole number, amounting to fifteen men, in order to get at their wives.

Shekurdin, shocked at these cruel proceedings, retired unperceived to the ship, and brought an account of all that had passed. Tsiuproff, instead of punishing these cruelties as they deserved, was secretly pleased with them; for he himself was affronted at the islanders for having refused to give him an iron bolt, which he saw in their possession. He had, in consequence of their refusal, committed several acts of hostilities against them; and had even formed the horrid design of poisoning them with a mixture of corrosive sublimate. In order, however, to preserve appearances, he dispatched Shekurdin and Nevodsikoff to re- proach Belayeff for his disorderly conduct ; but sent him, at the same time, by the above-men- tioned persons, more powder and ball.

The Russians continued upon this island, where they caught a large quantity of sea-otters, until the 14th of September, 1746 ; when, no longer thinking themselves secure, they put to sea with an intention of looking out for some uninhabited islands. Being, however, overtaken by a violent storm, they were driven about until the 30th of October, when their vessel struck upon a rocky shore, and was shipwrecked, with the loss of almost all the tackle, and the greatest part of the furs. Worn out at length with cold and fatigue, they ventured, the 1st of November, to penetrate into the interior part of the country, which they found rocky and uneven. Upon their coming to some huts, they were informed, that they were cast away upon the island of Karaga, the inhabitants of which were tributary to Russia, and of the Koraki tribe.   The islanders behaved to them with great kindness, until Belayeff had the imprudence to make proposals to the wife of the chief.   The woman gave immediate intelligence to her husband; and the natives were incensed to such a degree, that they threatened the whole crew with immediate death: but means were found to pacify them, and they continued to live with the Russians upon the same good terms as before.

The 30th of may, 1747, a party of Olotorians made a descent upon the island in three baidars, and attacked the natives ; but, after some loss on both sides, they went away.   They returned soon after with a larger force, and were again forced to retire.   But as they threatened to come again in a short time, and to destroy all the inhabitants who paid tribute, the latter advised the Russians to retire from the island, and assisted them in building two baidars, With these they put to sea on the 27th of June, and landed the 21st of July at Kamtchatka. with the rest of their cargo, consisting of 320 sea-otters, of which they paid the tenth into the customs. During this expedition twelve men were lost.

CHAP. XIII.

Successive voyages, from 1747 to 1753, to Beering's and the Aleütian Isles—some account of the inhabitants.

In the year 1747* two vessels sailed from the Kamtchatka river, according to a permission granted by the chancery of Bolcheresk for hunting sea-otters. One was fitted out by Andrew Wsevidoff, and carried forty-six men, besides eight Cossacks: the other belonged to Feodor Cholodiloff, Andrew Tolstyk, and company; and had on board a crew, consisting of forty-one Russians and Kamtchadals, with six Cossacks.

The latter vessel sailed the 20th of October, and was forced, by stress of weather and other

---

* It may be necessary to inform the reader, that, in this chapter, some circumstances are occasionally omitted, which are to be found in the original. These omissions relate chiefly to the names of some of the partners engaged in the equipments, and to a detail of immaterial occurrences prior to the actual departure of the vessels.

K

accidents, to winter in Beering's Island. From thence they departed May 31st, 1748, and touched at another small island, in order to provide themselves with water and other necessaries. They then steered S. E. for a considerable way without discovering any new islands; and, being in great want of provisions, returned into Kamtchatka river, August 14th, with a cargo of 250 old sea-otter skins, above 100 young ones, and 148 petsi, or Arctic fox-skins, which were all slain upon Beering's Island.

We have no sufficient account of Wsevidoff's voyage. All that is known amounts only to this, that he returned the 25th of July, 1749, after having probably touched upon one of the nearest Aleütian Isles which was uninhabited: his cargo consisted of the skins of 1040 sea-otters, and 2000 Arctic foxes.

Emilian Yugoff, a merchant of Yakutsk, obtained from the senate of St. Petersburg the permission of fitting out four vessels for himself and his associates. He procured, at the same time, the exclusive privilege of hunting sea-otters upon Beering's Island during these expeditions; and, for this monopoly, he agreed to deliver to the customs the tenth of the furs.

October 6th, 1750, he put to sea from Bolcheresk, in the sloop John, manned with twenty-five Russians and Kamtchadals, and two Cossacks: he was soon overtaken by a storm, and the vessel driven on shore between the mouths of the rivers Kronotsk and Tschasminsk.

October, 1751, he again set sail. He had been commanded to take on board some officers of the Russian Navy; and, as he disobeyed this injunction, the chancery of Irkutsk issued an order to confiscate his ship and cargo upon its return. The ship returned on the 22nd of July, 1754, to New Kamtchatkoi Ostrog, laden with the skins of 755 old sea-otters, of 35 cub sea-otters, of 447 cubs of sea-bears, and of 7044 Arctic fox-skins; of the latter, 2000 were white, and 1765 black. These furs were procured upon Beering's Island. Yugoff himself died at this island. The cargo of the ship was, according to the above-mentioned order, sealed and properly secured. But, as it appeared that certain persons had deposited money in Yugoff's hands, for the purpose of equipping a second vessel, the Crown delivered up the confiscated cargo, after reserving the third part, according to the original stipulation.

This kind of charter-company, if it may be so called, being soon dissolved, for misconduct and want of sufficient stock, other merchants were allowed the privilege of fitting out vessels, even before the return of Yugoff's ship; and these persons were more fortunate, in making new discoveries, than the above-mentioned monopolist.

Nikiphor Trapesnikoff, a merchant of Irkutsk, obtained the permission of sending out a ship, called the Boris and Glebb, upon the condition of paying, besides the tribute which might be exacted, the tenth of all the furs. The Cossack, Sila Sheffyrin, went on board this vessel for the purpose of collecting the tribute. They sailed in August, 1749, from the Kamtchatka river; and re-entered it the 16th of the same month, 1753, with a large cargo of furs. In the spring of the same year, they had touched upon an unknown island, probably one of the Aleütians, were several of the inhabitants were prevailed upon to pay a tribute of sea-otter skins. The names of the islanders who had been made tributary, were Igya, Oeknu, Ogogoektack, Shabukiauck, Alak, Tutun, Ononushan. Rotogèi, Tschinitu, Vatsch, Ashagat, Avyjanishaga, Unashayupu, Lak, Yanshugalik, Umgalikan, Shati, Kyipago, and Oloshkot;* another Aleütian had contributed three sea-otters. They brought with them 320 best sea-otter skins, 480 of the second, and 400 of the third sort; 500 female and middle-aged, and 220 Medwedki or young ones.

Andrew Tolstyk, a merchant of Selengensk, having obtained permission from the chancery

---

* The author here remarks in a note, that the proper names of the islanders mentioned in this place, and in other parts, bear a surprising resemblance, both in their sound and termination, to those of the Greenlanders.

of Bolcheresk, refitted the same ship which had made a former voyage; he sailed from Kamtchatka August the 19th, 1749, and returned July the 3rd, 1752.

According to the commander's account, the ship lay at anchor from the 6th of September, 1749, to the 20th of May, 1750, before Beering's Island, where they caught only 47 sea-otters. From thence they made to those Aleütian Islands, which were first discovered by Nevodtsikoff, and slew there 1662 old and middled-aged sea-otters, and 119 cubs; besides which, their cargo consisted of the skins of 720 blue foxes, and of 840 sea-bears.

The inhabitants of these islands appeared to have never before paid tribute; and seemed to be akin to the Tschutkski tribe, their women being ornamented with different figures sewed into the skin in the manner of that people, and of the Tungusians of Siberia. They differed, however, from them, by having two small holes cut through the bottom of their under lips, through each of which they pass a bit of the sea-horse tusk, worked into the form of a tooth, with a small button at one end to keep it within the mouth when it is placed in the hole. They had killed, without being provoked, two of the Kamtchadals who belonged to the ship. Upon the third island some inhabitants had payed tribute; their names were reported to be Anitin, Altakukor, and Aleshkut, with his son Atschelap. The weapons of the whole island consisted of no more than twelve spears pointed with flint, and one dart of bone pointed with the same; and the Russians observed in the possession of the natives two figures, carved out of wood, resembling sea-lions.

August 3, 1750, the vessel Simeon and John, fitted out by the above-mentioned Wsevidoff, agent for the Russian merchant, A. Rybenskoi, and manned with fourteen Russians (who were partly merchants and partly hunters) and thirty Kamtchadals, sailed out for the discovery of new islands, under the command of the Cossack Vorobieff. They were driven by a violent current and tempestuous weather to a small desert island, whose position is not determined; but which was probably one of those that lie near Beering's Island. The ship being so shattered by the storm, that it was no longer in a condition to keep the sea, Vorobieff built another small vessel with drift-wood, which he called Jeremiah; in which he arrived at Kamtchatka in Autumn, 1752.

Upon the above-mentioned island were caught 700 old and 120 cub sea-otters, 1900 blue foxes, 5700 black sea bears, and 1310 Kotiki, or cub sea-bears.

The trade between Kamtchatka, the last mentioned islands, and several other islands situated close to the continent of North West America, was carried on with great success for several years; at length the animals became exceedingly scarce, on account of the dams being indiscriminately slaughtered by the Russian huntsmen, the cubs were left to perish for the want of proper nurture. Individual enterprize was withdrawn on this account from the trade, finding it to be no longer profitable.

Towards the close of the last century, a company was formed at St. Petersburg, under a royal charter, to carry on this once profitable branch of commerce ;—the company was styled " The Royal American Company of Russia." Success attended the company's undertakings in those seas, up to the year 1814 ;—since that time it has been gradually decreasing, as the animals have become exceedingly scarce. At present the produce of the trade barely pays the company's expenses.

It is rumoured, that the company will be obliged, shortly, to abandon their charter. Report says, that the Imperial Government will take charge of the new settlements and colonies, founded by the company on some of the islands, and on the continent of North West America, near to Cook's Inlet and Nootka Sound.

In 1839, the sea-otter skins from Kamtchatka realized enormous prices, at the annual fairs of Kiachta, the supply not being sufficient to meet the demand.

For EU product safety concerns, contact us at Calle de José Abascal, 56–1°, 28003 Madrid, Spain or eugpsr@cambridge.org.